MEDITATIONS AND ASCENSIONS

MEDITATIONS AND ASCENSIONS

BLACK WRITERS ON WRITING

Edited by

Brenda M. Greene and Fred Beauford

Third World Press
Chicago

Third World Press
Publishers since 1967
Chicago

First Edition
Printed in the United States of America

Cover design by Bernie Rollins
Inside text layout and design by Relana Johnson

Library of Congress Cataloging-in-Publication Data

Meditations and ascensions : Black writers on writing / edited by Brenda M.
Greene and Fred Beauford. — 1st ed.
    p. cm.
  "This publication is an outgrowth of the Eighth National Black Writers
Conference, "Black Literature: Expanding Conversations on Race, Identity, History
and Genre", which was sponsored by the Center for Black Literature at Medgar
Evers College from March 30 through April 2, 2006"—Introd.
  Includes bibliographical references and index.
  ISBN-13: 978-0-88378-296-5 (alk. paper)
  ISBN-10: 0-88378-296-0 (alk. paper)
1. American literature—African American authors—History and criticism—
Congresses. 2. African American authors—Biography—Congresses. 3.
Authorship—Congresses. 4. African Americans in literature—Congresses. 5. Race
in literature—Congresses. 6. African Americans—Race identity—Congresses. I.
Greene, Brenda M., 1950- II. Beauford, Fred.
  PS153.N5M38 2008
  810'.9'896073—dc22
                                    2008007793

12 11 10 09 08   6 5 4 3 2 1

CONTENTS

CHAPTER SIX   93
Speculative Fiction
> *Robert Reid-Pharr, Samuel Delany, Tananarive Due,*
> *Sheree Renée Thomas, and Walter Mosley*

CHAPTER SEVEN   123
The Writer as Literary and Cultural Artist
> *Carlos Russell, Steven Barnes, Carl Hancock Rux, and*
> *Camille Yarbrough*

CHAPTER EIGHT   151
Reflections on the Creative Writing Process
> *Valerie Wilson Wesley interviewed by Richard Wesley*

CHAPTER NINE   163
Art and Politics in Publishing
> *Linda Duggins, Tonya M. Evans, Malaika Adero, and*
> *Manie Barron*

FOREWORD
Myrlie Evers-Williams

It's not an easy job, but this community has shown by developing the very concept of Medgar Evers College that they have what it takes to make a success of an institution that helps to shape the minds and hearts of so many young people—and those who are not so young—who come through these doors. It's all about building leadership. It's about giving a sense of history and what better place to have this National Conference of Black Writers than at Medgar Evers College?

I want to share with you what I learned from my grandmother and my aunt. They would always tell me that books would serve as a way to open doors to places that I would not be able to go. Books could take me to places that I could not imagine, allow me to meet people that I would not have met, or would not be able to meet otherwise. I could sit someplace quietly with a book and transform my life. I could become someone else that I read about, or I could develop a vision of who I was, and learn who my people were, the contributions that they made and, in so doing, be able to have a sense of pride about who I was.

I was fortunate during that time also to have teachers. Teachers who said long before Jesse Jackson made it popular, "I am somebody." Those wise teachers gave to us books where sometimes the pages were torn out; but they gave to us something else. A sense of who we were, a sense of what we could become and the responsibility to live up to what was expected of us.

For young girls growing up in a segregated society who

only once a year found themselves privy to a small selection of books that talked about Marian Anderson, Booker T. Washington, and a few others, we knew the importance of books. We would read their stories, relive their lives and hoped to be like them. Those books were our treasures. Perhaps one of the most powerful things that we have as human beings is not only the spoken word, but the written word that lasts forever.

There was a time not too long ago in the early 1970s when the major publishing companies said there is no market for books about Blacks and books by Blacks, "because most of you don't read anyway." And unfortunately, I know that to be true, because when I attempted to have my first book published, *For Us the Living*, I was told by the publishers and the publicists that they did not know what market there was for the book.

For those who have persevered, who have even self-published your books, you are to be praised for your vision, for your abilities and for reaching out.

I am so pleased to have been asked to be the Honorary Chair of this Eighth Conference. I wish you well. I embrace all that you do because in your books we learn not only about ourselves, but about others and we provide an opportunity for those who think they know us, to find out who we really are and what we are capable of.

ACKNOWLEDGEMENTS

This publication, *Meditations and Ascensions: Black Writers on Writing*, is the result of the Eighth National Conference at Medgar Evers College of the City University of New York. The Conference was made possible because of the contributions and collective work of our Conference team, our partnering organizations, and our public and private sponsors.

I am especially thankful to Medgar Evers College and the support of President Edison O. Jackson for providing me with the time and resources to direct the National Black Writers Conference. The Conference team included Subhannah Wahhaj, April Silver, Julia Shaw, Maeshay Lewis, Steven Nardi, Susan McHenry, Beatrice Brathwaite, Keisha Green, Gregory Pardlo, Michelle Davidson, Jennifer Sparrow, and Richard Jones.

My sponsors and partners were invaluable and this Conference could not have been held without them. They include the National Endowment for the Arts, Barnes and Noble, the College Now Program of the Office of Academic Affairs, the Gladys Krieble Delmas Foundation, Con Edison, the Ford Foundation, Time Warner, the African American Literary Book Club (AALBC), St. Paul's Community Baptist Church, the *New York Times* and Little, Brown, and Company.

Haki Madhubuti, Founder and CEO of Third World Press, offered to publish these proceedings when he delivered his talk at the Conference. I thank him for his foresight and commitment to the work of Black writers. I also thank my co-editor, Fred Beauford, for his persistence and determination to ensure the publication of this manuscript.

Meditations and Ascensions: Black Writers on Writing represents the voices of many writers. They are our conscience and our griots. They remind us of the past, comment on the present, and envision the future. I thank them for their work and in the words of John Oliver Killens, founder of the first National Black Writers Conference at Medgar Evers College, for being "long distance runners."

INTRODUCTION

Brenda M. Greene

This book, *Meditations and Ascensions: Black Writers on Writing,* is an outgrowth of the Eighth National Black Writers Conference, "Black Literature: Expanding Conversations on Race, Identity, History and Genre" which was sponsored by the Center for Black Literature at Medgar Evers College from March 30 through April 2, 2006. The National Black Writers Conference, currently a major program of the Center for Black Literature, has been held at Medgar Evers College since 1986.

The title of this book, *Meditations and Ascensions* is taken from two albums composed by the late John Coltrane. The two albums, *Meditations* and *Ascension* reflect a shift to what became an avante garde jazz movement, one which was called by some "provocative, intense, ferocious, and passionate." Coltrane composed these albums at about the same time that he married the late Alice Coltrane, a marriage which embodied a strong spiritual and musical connection between these two legendary jazz artists. *Meditations and Ascensions* pays tribute to them and is a testament to the value of acknowledging transition and embracing change.

Like music, the themes, forms, structures, and voices in literature are continually evolving, expanding, and shifting. Just as Coltrane's *Meditations* and *Ascension* represented radical shifts in the jazz movement, the discussion that emerged from the Conference reveals a shift in the kinds of conversations that Black writers and conference attendees had with respect to representations of history, identity, race, and genre. The writers in this book meditate on the state of black literature and pose paths of ascension for its future. *Meditations and Ascensions: Black Writers on Writing* is their story and testament.

The Center for Black Literature

The Center for Black Literature at Medgar Evers College was established in 2003 to continue the tradition and legacy of the National Black Writers Conference, to serve as a voice, mecca, and resource for Black writers, and to study the impact of black literature on our society. It is the only Center in the country primarily devoted to supporting Black writers and the literature they produce.

The literature produced by Black writers is multi-faceted and complicated; it is a literature that expresses the history, hopes, fears, and challenges of a people who have come from various parts of the African diaspora and who have endured the realities of living in societies constructed by race and class. These experiences have affected the literature of Black writers in myriad ways. Hence, because the themes that Black writers address are constantly evolving and cannot easily be defined by static categories, the general reading public has had to rethink and reexamine its notions and definitions of the literature produced by Black writers.

Through its conferences, symposia, retreats, and educational programs, the Center for Black Literature sets the stage for ongoing critical conversations on the literature produced by Black writers from aesthetic, historical, social, and political perspectives. It examines the impact of this literature on readers and writers and posits future directions for black literature. Its target audience is intergenerational and includes the literary world: writers, editors, agents, and publishers, the general public, educators, and readers and writers at the elementary and high school level.

Through its work with local and national literary, educational, and cultural programs, organizations, and institutions, the Center for Black Literature has had an impact on several thousand people each year. In addition to sponsoring the National Black Writers Conference, the Center sponsors the Re-Envisioning Our Lives through Literature High School Collaborative Project, the North Country Institute and Retreat for Writers of Color, a radio program *Writers on Writing*, and an Elder African American Writers Workshop. Additional programs sponsored by the Center have included the Brother to Brother Literary Symposium: symposia on Calvin Hernton, John Oliver Killens, and Gwendolyn Brooks: a writer in residency program with Sonia Sanchez, and author readings and signings. Writers who have participated in these programs include Tony Medina, Ethelbert Miller, Sandra Jackson-Opoku, Patrice Gaines, Martin Espada, Jose Torres, Kenji Jasper, Ruby Dee, Ossie Davis, Kevin Powell, Elizabeth Alexander, Gloria Naylor, and Alexs Pate among others.

The National Black Writers Conference

Inspired by the late John Oliver Killens, the first National Black Writers Conference was initially convened over a period of four days to bring together writers, critics, booksellers, book reviewers, and the general public in order to establish a dialogue on the social responsibility of the Black writer. Since 1986, subsequent conferences (1988, 1991, 1996, 2000, 2003, and 2004) have included discussions on stereotypes in black literature, the direction of black literature, the renaissance in black literature, the impact of black literature on society, and literature as access. The Seventh National Conference in 2004 was a symposium and tribute on the late John Oliver Killens. Peter Lang published the proceedings of the Fifth National Conference in 1998, *Defining Ourselves: Black Writers in the 90s*. The Center for Black Literature published the proceedings of the Sixth and Seventh Conferences, *And Then They Heard Our Thunder*, Volumes I and II, in 2003 and 2004.

The National Black Writers Conferences have attracted writers and scholars such as Maya Angelou, Houston Baker, Amiri Baraka, Fred Beauford, Toni Cade Bambara, Octavia Butler, Colin Channer, Samuel Delany, Michael Eric Dyson, Henry Louis Gates Jr., Marita Golden, Haki R. Madhubuti, Paule Marshall, Walter Dean Myers, Walter Mosley, Elizabeth Nunez, Fred Beauford, Arnold Rampersad, Ishmael Reed, Carl Hancock Rux, Quincy

Troupe, Sonia Sanchez, Alice Walker, Margaret Walker, and John Edgar Wideman among others.

Meditations and Ascensions: Black Writers on Writing

This book, a representation of conversations from the Eighth National Black Writers Conference, reflects the ways in which the literature currently being written by Black writers reexamines history from alternative perspectives, expands notions of identity, reshapes the forms and structures used to create literature, and draws upon an increasingly diverse readership. The conference participants explored the following issues: the ways in which multiculturalism, diversity, and plurality impact the literature produced by Black writers; the ways in which Black writers reflect and portray the complexity of the American identity; the ways in which Black writers represent and frame race; the ways in which historical texts by Black writers affirm, reject, and depict the racial history of this nation and the world; the ways in which Black writers have used speculative fiction to create alternative realities; and Black writers' views on future directions for black literature. The conversations that emerged from the discussions of these issues provided the public and broader literary community with more in-depth analyses of the ways in which the literature created by Black writers reflects the black experience, the American experience, and a more global experience and worldview.

Black Literature: Expanding Conversations on Race, Identity, History and Genre

Ishmael Reed, a featured writer on the panel: "The Paradox of Race and Identity in Literature by Black Writers" ended his presentation with a quotation from the American poet, T.S. Eliot: "All ethnic writers might not be great, but all great writers are ethnic." This quotation provides a context for examining an emerging and recurring theme throughout all of the conference panels: "History as Narrative in Literature by Black Writers"; "The

Paradox of Race and Identity in Literature by Black Writers";
"Speculative Fiction"; "The Black Writer as Literary and Cultural
Artist"; and "Publishers, Editors, and Agents on Publishing Black
Literature." The theme reiterates the concept that although
distinctions between identity and race have become more blurred,
and in some cases have collapsed, the Black writer, in writing from
the point of view of specificity, is writing from his/her experience,
which is inevitably a Black, or if you will, an ethnic experience,
and which is also a human and universal experience.

A paradox emerges, however, when others refuse to accept
the complexity of the characters in a particular text, and instead
expect to see only stereotypical depictions of those characters,
thereby creating as Emily Raboteau, another writer on this panel
reminds us: a situation where the only books by Black writers
considered marketable are those whose characters are portrayed
with certain ethnic traits. This panel also raised the issues in
Percival Edward's *Erasure*, a well crafted satire of a Black man
who plays to the public's appetite for "urban street fiction" in order
to get published, not unlike the best selling author Zane, whose
writing career was really launched when she decided to focus on
writing erotica and subsequently made millions of dollars for
herself and for Atria books, the company that publishes her.

This theme, the value of writing from a particular
experience, is also epitomized in the keynote speech by Marita
Golden who declares that she has never written from the margins
and that neither race nor gender has shackled her as a writer.
Rather, she has assumed the power of authority as a writer, as an
"author," and hence writes from the authority of an African
American woman who must recover the complexity and banish the
one-dimensional representations of her character.

Haki Madhubuti continues this theme of writers as writing
from a particular experience when he talks about the value of
"layering yourself with the knowledge of yourself, your history,
and your culture." The layering of knowledge paves the way for
individuals to become successful with any journey or path on

which they embark. In so doing, they arm themselves with the tools and knowledge for self-determination and for taking ownership of themselves, their family, and their community.

Carl Hancock Rux, a writer on the "Writer as Literary and Cultural Artist" panel, introduces the concept of the writer who interrogates himself and in the process "invades his own privacy." This writer, who also writes from the perspective of one who is layered in knowledge, is positioned to create narratives steeped in truth, narratives such as the "Liberation Narratives" that Haki Madhubuti argues are necessary for young people, narratives that have substance and provide direction.

The act of writing from one's cultural and specific experience and the layering of one's self with knowledge are also reiterated in the conference panel on the "History as Narrative in the Literature by Black Writers." Valerie Boyd, a writer on this panel, calls upon those who are interested in writing and those who want to be history makers, to draw upon an untapped area of exploration in recounting the history of Black people. She suggests that writers who take up this task can recount this history in one of two ways: through historical fiction that uses imagination to recreate or to tell the story of a historical person or event that is grounded in fact, or through creative nonfiction that presents a true account of a historical event or person through the use of elements of creative writing; the challenge in either case is to tell a story that is engaging to the reader.

Writers from the Speculative Fiction panel discuss how the use of ethnic and layered experiences provides writers with opportunities to create alternative realities where the imagination is free to depict black characters in time and space not formerly encountered. Walter Mosley calls science fiction or speculative fiction the truly revolutionary fiction, a fiction that is in particular a natural genre for a place of ideas about the imagined future, present, and past for Black people.

Panelists from the "Publishers, Editors, and Agents on Publishing Black Literature" session discuss the politics of

xvi

publishing. They note that assumptions about race and identity abound and continue to haunt and shadow Black writers and the literature they produce, thus causing those who are not perceived as writing from a black or ethnic experience to be marginalized and silenced in the book publishing and book selling industry. However, they argue that these dilemmas are not new and that because publishing is a business, publishers and the bookselling industry will support the publishing and selling of those books they see as commercially viable. In short, publishers are cautious about increasing the quantity and range of "literary books" by Black writers because they do not see the demand for these books.

Manie Barron, an agent for the Menza Literary Agency, and Maliaka Adero, Senior Editor for Atria Books, an imprint of Simon and Schuster, challenge the reading public to respond to publishers in different ways. They note that publishers take the lead of the public and if the reading public wants to see more books of a "higher" literary nature published, the publishers will respond to the public's demand. Barron and Adero also point out that there is no reason to support one type of text over another; many texts can coexist because reading interests vary. They stress that there is a need for more dialogue and conversations concerning the ways in which the publishing industry can meet the reading needs of a more eclectic and diverse Black readership. Hence they remind the conference attendees that an ongoing challenge for readers and writers is to take a leadership role in shaping the kinds of books that will be published.

Chapter Overview: *Meditations and Ascensions: Black Writers on Writing*

The book is divided into nine chapters and opens with a foreword by the Honorary Chair of the Eighth National Black Writers Conference, Dr. Myrlie Evers-Williams. Dr. Evers-Williams shares the way in which books have enriched her life and the lives of her peers. She describes how the stories of Black heroes and sheroes were motivational and inspired her and those around her to live productive lives and made them want to relive the lives of those about whom they had read. She also praises those who have the vision to publish and cautions them to persist rather than be deterred when they are told that there is no market for their books.

Marita Golden, in her keynote speech on "Voice, Authority, and the Writer," portrays the powerful people in her life, her parents as the ones who shaped and affirmed her as a writer and who provided her with the authority to write. She describes how her father's rich stories and her mother's naming of her as a writer allowed her to dream and construct her own identity as a writer whose writing self has been shaped by her background and experiences as an African American female growing up in this society. Golden discusses the subjects of her books in more detail in her interview with Susan McHenry. In this section, Chapter Two in this book, she addresses issues such as the killing of a young man by a Black police officer, the subject of her novel *After*; colorism in the Black community, the subject of her non fiction book *Don't Play in the Sun*; and cultural conflicts and single parenting, major subjects in her autobiographical narrative *Migrations of the Heart.*

Haki Madhubuti's talk in Chapter Three provides a roadmap of his life. Beginning with a story of the obstacles he faced in starting a charter school in Chicago, he recounts how he has survived, despite growing up in poverty and surrounded by drugs, prostitution, and violence. Madhubuti reads two poems, which are testaments to the important values in his life, one on the responsibility of the poet and one on the value of art for young people. In passionate and inspiring prose, he describes how the combination of his knowledge gained from books, art, and mentors provided him with self-determination and how this combination can also provide others with the power to transform their lives and the lives of those around them. He notes that this transformative process is accomplished through immersing one's self in a consciousness of culture.

Chapter Four on "History as Narrative" focuses on the way

in which the history of Black people has not been presented comprehensively and on the scarcity of historical texts written by Black people. The panelists note that much has been left out and distorted, and that this can be addressed by having Black writers tell their own stories. Valerie Boyd calls for writers to take up the mantle of delving into untapped waters and providing a historical and cultural perspective that will assist readers in connecting to texts in ways that they have not previously connected, while Christopher John Marley emphasizes the need for more Black writers who will tell the truth and provide detailed facts and accurate information about the history of Black people.

The writers Elizabeth Nunez, Mohammad N. Ali, Emily Raboteau, and Ishmael Reed, from the panel on "The Paradox of Race and Identity" pose questions related to the publisher's, bookseller's and general public's expectation that Black writers should only write about subjects related to race. They note that publishers will often tell them that their book is not marketable if it does not directly relate to race; booksellers will place their books in African American literature sections solely on the basis of their race; and the general public has been trained by the book selling industry to go to the African American literature section to find books written by Black writers. Thus, the availability of, and access to books by Black writers are limited by the publishing and bookselling industries. The writers on this panel recommend that those who want to publish expand their potential publishing options and seek alternative venues such as independent presses, the internet, and so forth.

Chapter Six on "Speculative Fiction" is dedicated to the memory of Octavia Butler, and with wit, love, and grace, the legendary science fiction writer, Samuel Delany opens this panel by recounting how he met Butler when she was a student in his class and how they continued to inspire each other as colleagues and friends throughout the years. Sheree Renee Thomas continues the tribute to Butler with a moving portrayal of her encounter with Butler. Thomas then describes her foray into "speculative fiction," how this was the fiction that she read to gain ideas, and how she was motivated to create two anthologies on speculative fiction by Black writers. Tananarive Due and Walter Mosley also reflect on the influence of Butler's life on their lives and on their work.

In Chapter Seven, dedicated to August Wilson, "The Black Writer as Literary and Cultural Artist," Steven Barnes, Carl Hancock Rux, and Camille Yarbrough discuss the multidimensional role of the artist. They focus on the concept of the literary, visual, performing, and cultural arts as powerful platforms for sharing one's history, healing the community and assisting people in becoming agents of change. Carl Hancock Rux notes that art is enhanced rather than reduced when the artist is able to work in more than one medium. The artist, Steven Barnes notes, gives to the world something that is not seen.

Valerie Wilson Wesley is interviewed by her husband, playwright and screenwriter, Richard Wesley in Chapter Eight. In an engaging and warm manner, Richard questions Valerie on her writing process, on the process she uses to create her characters in a various genres: mysteries, children's literature and novels, on the themes she chooses to write about and on her writing muses and mentors.

The final chapter in this book, "The Politics and Art of Publishing" provides the perspectives of an agent, editor, and book publisher. Using Nick Child's essay, "Their Eyes Were Reading Smut," which was published by the *New York Times*, moderator Linda Duggins, asks the panelists about the future directions for writers and publishers of black literature. In a frank and heated discussion, the panelists lay out the issues from the perspective of the industry and challenge the readers to take responsibility in shaping the future of publishing for Black writers.

The conversations about writing and literature that emerged from this conference embodied the ways in which definitions about race, identity, history, and genre are being redefined through the kinds of texts Black writers create and in the ways they talk about writing. These writers resist being pigeonholed and assume the authority to compose texts that both speak to their own particular experiences and that cross the lines of race, ethnicity, and genre. Although they live in a society socially constructed by race, their texts, both fiction and nonfiction, speak to issues about race and transcend race, issues such as fear, poverty, survival, violence, war, immigration, love, birth, death, spirituality, and so forth.

By virtue of the fact that they are Black writers, their stories are shaped by their experiences as Black individuals and reflective of the experiences of "others" in real and imagined worlds. As writers, they are the truth tellers, the griots, the conscience, and the courageous voices of the world. The need for dialogue concerning the value of their voices is paramount if we realize their authority as writers, the redemptive power of their writing, and the ways in which they are redefining boundaries, presenting the public with expanded realities, and using writing in new and innovative ways. Their ongoing challenge is to convince readers to ask for and support more texts that illustrate and depict the complexity of the black experience.

MEDITATIONS AND ASCENSIONS

CHAPTER ONE
Who Said You Could Say That? Voice, Authority and the Writer

Marita Golden

This chapter represents Golden's reflections on writing from the perspective of an African American woman in American society. She provides a vivid portrait of her journey to acquiring voice and authority. Golden is the author of 12 books of fiction and nonfiction. Her essays have appeared in numerous journals. In her most recent book of essays, Don't Play In the Sun: One Woman's Journey Through the Color Complex *(2004), Golden conducts a self-analysis that reveals the psychological and social effects from the negative ideology that comes with being a woman of dark skin. She also examines the media and the entertainment entity's neglect and the cynical sentiment for people with heightened melanin. Her journey is accompanied by testaments from friends, colleagues, and experts who agree that the world has been seasoned with this artificial perception of people who are blessed with excess melanin.*

I have spent a lot of time thinking about writing from a technical perspective. Is this chapter effective? Is this description compelling? But I wanted to take a deep breath and really think about how in the world I had gotten the nerve to write twelve books. Who told me I could do that and how had I gotten the authority, the personal authority to do that? Because this business of writing is an absolutely breathtaking, awesome, scary endeavor and every time we sit down to attempt it, we are actually stepping out on faith.

So I wanted to think about where I had gotten my faith, and how I had gotten my sense of authority, because I think that long before the author published a book, something tells us, or somebody has told us that we're supposed to speak, and that we're supposed to be heard.

I begin with a kind of internal dialogue. The first person to formally anoint me with a sense of literary authority was my mother. This powerful act of designation and faith was performed in the kitchen one afternoon as I watched her make biscuits. My mother raised her eyes from the circular mound of dough, her hands coated in flour, and looked at me in a slyly offhand manner that in no way hinted at the momentousness of what she was about to say. She whispered as though sharing some long held secret, "One day, you're going to write a book."

Shakespeare said that all power lies in the world of dreams. My mother had watched me, her youngest, daydreaming, poetry writing, book devouring daughter and observed my hunger both to consume the world and to recreate it. Of all the things my mother ever said to me, that charge, that prediction, has come over the years to resonate as I repeat it silently or loudly, with more love than perhaps any other words she ever spoke to me. "One day, you're going to write a book." Imagine how much confidence a mother must possess in her child in order to offer her such an assignment.

My mother had given birth to me twelve years earlier, and that day in our kitchen, she gave birth to me again. She saw through me, bored into my soul, and interpreted my dreams. She articulated for me a vision that was impossible for me to assert for myself. It is one thing to dream of a desire; it is quite another to lay claim to it with language. My mother became an architect of a house, a space, a place that I've lived in unconsciously and consciously most of my life.

When I'm asked to name the major influences of my writing career, without hesitation I always cite my parents— Francis and Beatrice Golden. They were the kind of parents that girls who grew up to be authors are supposed to have, because of the inspiring drama of their lives. A father who dropped out of school in the sixth grade and then proceeded to educate himself, who was charismatic and Afrocentric long before the term was coined. A father who sat on my bed in the dark as I huddled beneath the spreads and blankets and told me bedtime stories of the exploits of Cleopatra and Hannibal and Sojourner Truth, and who became my first writing teacher, introducing me to the basics of good storytelling in these narratives about larger than life people I could never forget, people I dreamed about when my father had left my room and I closed my eyes. A father who treated me as though I was his son, not his daughter by taking me into the farthest reaches of his man world, from basements where he shot dice to afternoons in the front seat as he ferried passengers all over Washington D.C. in his taxi. A father who was vain and arrogant, willful and proud and who gave me much to overcome and whose love was a crucible and, in the end, a form of redemption.

There was my mother who loved hard and dreamed big. Who went from domestic worker to the owner of half a dozen boarding houses in the space of a few years after she migrated from Greensboro, North Carolina, to Washington D.C. in the 1920s. She was a woman of opposites and contradictions. Her first husband was so light he had on occasion passed for white. Her second husband, my father, was black as coal. She was too impatient to read much, be it newspapers or books, preferring to be surrounded by friends, seated at a table laden with food. The cacophony of laughter, jokes in dozens, her theme music, but she gave me a subscription to *The New York Times* for my eighteenth birthday and called me a writer before anyone else ever did.

My mother named me twice. Once on the day I was born, then again when she recognized my gift. In naming me the second time, she bestowed upon me a sense of my personal authority to speak, imagine and create. Authority is always illusive, not just because I was an African-American and a woman. The society that shaped me was designed to deny me any sense of authority; authority is elusive for everyone. For if we are human, we have been silenced. We have been muted. Our tongues somewhere have been tied.

I owe the beginnings of my writing career to my parents for vastly different reasons. My father nurtured my imagination with the stories that he told me and instilled in me a sense that I should exist and live without bonds.

Toni Morrison has said that the ability of writers to familiarize the strange and mystify the familiar is a test of their power. Because my father taught me that nothing in my mind and no place in the world was out of reach to me, I was introduced early on to the possibilities and seductions of the strange and the familiar. Perhaps because my father opened the mysteries of his world to me, I found myself so often a sojourner and a pilgrim in other lands, literally and figuratively, trying to master a new language and turn it into a mother tongue. Perhaps because my father bestowed on me night after night, like some black Shaharazad, the stories of my ancestors, I could imagine myself mastering the strange, unnatural act of writing.

While my father's lessons were subtle, I cherish the memory of my mother's directness. She had catapulted herself from the small shotgun house where she was born and raised, into a three story Victorian property that we called home, and she had done it without much education, armed with a savvy cultural literacy that enabled her to read the writing on the wall; to see which way the wind was blowing; to trust her instincts and to compose a personal script that climaxed with her own personal happy ending. She had done all that. I was her daughter, who holed up in the attic reading Jane Austen and Dickens in the summer. Her daughter, who some said was so different from her because of the love of books and reading, but the daughter that she knew better than anyone else. The daughter who she could see was inventing herself in bits and pieces and who only needed someone to say the words, to tell her what it was indeed, possible to do.

My parents grabbed life by the handful, striding through their existence like giants, whose every footstep set convention trembling and searching for a place to hide from their ravenous reach. Their model of self-invention was brazen and honored the most ancient traditions of the artist and the writer. They lived their lives like poets, or jazz musicians, improvising a new way to be free with their choices, which rang throughout my life and theirs like an unheralded but magnificent symphony. Somehow, some way, my parents had claimed for themselves the authority to believe their dreams into reality, and they raised me to believe that I could write my way into an existence beyond anything they could imagine.

The word authority is rooted in the word author. An author is someone who seeks not merely to write, but to write with a conscious sense of attempting to shake the known world to its core—the known world of their imagination, the known world of manners, discourse—the known world of relationships between individuals, or between individuals and society—the known world that obscures what the writer is often terrified to discover and reveal to others, and yet what she must discover and reveal in order not only to write, but in order to live.

The often-reverent attitude with which we approach writers and the act of writing, especially those writers in those texts that challenge us, is rooted in the desire we all have to live with and find a sense of authority. We expect writers to speak up, to speak first, and to speak boldly because of the responsibility and the freedom inherent in authorizing oneself to use words.

The writers who have embedded themselves in our hearts, generation after generation, have most often spoken the unspeakable and walked over the burning coals of history's legacy, its pride and its shame. Readers know that these writers have walked over their coals in their place, and so we must bear witness to their courage, which is what we remember most, and require of great writers, courage born of a grand and serene sense of authority. The men and women who at this very moment all over the world are sitting before a computer screen, writing on a legal pad, facing the blank page, working up the courage to pick up a pen to write a novel or any kind of book do so not so much for riches or for fame, but for a sense of their own voice, their own authentic existence. They're seeking to bring themselves into being in the world and in relationship to others in a way that is utterly irresistible.

The personal authority constantly mutates and changes and challenges the person doomed and destined to write as a way of living in this world. My parents proved that we're all writers, scrawling our epitaph on the walls around us, some days like an angry anguished graffiti, other days with the precision of a prayer. While my parents were the first to give me a sense of my own personal and literary authority, I have had to battle nearly every day to maintain my belief in that authority. I've battled in my own cowardice and have been lucky enough to work with a few editors who would accept nothing less than everything that was possible in my construction and imagination of a text.

Then there is the fear that accompanies the creation of a book that is as natural and necessary a part of the process as the fact that you over come it. Each attempt to write is virginal, death defying and of course that is part of its attraction, that it tests us in so many ways. And yet so much of the authority of the writer is vested in her by readers who wrest the book from the writer's grip and define it, make of it what they will, mythologize it, shroud it in legend, construct and deconstruct it, swear on it like a Bible and throw it across the room in frustration and content.

Would Zora Neale Hurston recognize *Their Eyes Were*

Watching God as the book that she wrote after reading contemporary critical analysis of the text? Quite frankly, in the largest sense of what literary creation is about, Hurston's reaction to her readers' dialogue on the book means very little. In writing the book, she presented us not with a stagnant brittle tablet, but with an object as resilient as clay and as hearty as steel. Hurston did not need readers to write her masterpiece; even as it is, readers render unto the book its epitaph.

In *Their Eyes Were Watching God*, Zora Neale Hurston gave us a task that was colossal while the consciousness of the world when we first met the book was too small, too timid to embrace it. Not until the civil rights movement, the feminist movement, not until the Academy opened itself to the vision of women and men of color, was there enough intelligence in the world, not just to read the text, but to submit to it, to allow it to invade and alter us. These social changes belatedly authorized, and validated a human holistic vision of Black people and Black culture that Hurston legitimized decades before just by writing them down.

Hurston, of course, was authorized by her mother who told her to "jump at the sun." She was authorized by the people of Eatonville and by her own restless spirit. Readers, publishers, critics, teachers, and students of a writer's work all in various ways extend authority to the writer and endanger the writer's authority.

Everything I write is culled from the authority of my specific and unique experience as an African American. With each word, I'm trying to recover the complex and banish the one-dimensional, to create the surprising and essential in my experience as a Black female of the human family. For me, the act of writing as an author, of authoring my voice, my culture, is an act of treason I commit against the status quo every time I sit down to write.

And despite the oft-repeated popular literary theories, I have never, ever written from the margins. When I pick up my pen I aim for dead center, the heart of the matter, the heart of all experience. My race does not shackle me. My gender is no jail cell. For me, writing and literature are not luxuries, but necessities.

Our true home in history is contained in literature, be it the Declaration of Independence, the Emancipation Proclamation, Walt Whitman's *Leaves of Grass*, or Douglass' autobiography of slavery.

The act of writing and its product—literature—authorizes empathy, hatred, charity or war. Literature is inherently dangerous, conspiratorial, a necessity; it is at odds with internal and external controls. Who but the writer, who but the artist can really inform us of the true depths of what we have borne, dare imagine a holiness we have yet to claim? In the final analysis, the act of writing needs no authority. It is its own metaphor, its own definition in its contrariness and its unpredictability, its loyalty and its daring. Writing and literature create us as individuals and as people over and over again.

CHAPTER TWO
Reflections on Race, Colorism, and Identity

Marita Golden interviewed by Susan McHenry

Marita Golden: My latest novel, *After: A Novel,* was inspired by a young man named Prince Jones. He was a Howard University student in Washington D.C. and one night, he was followed by an undercover Black officer from Washington D.C. through Maryland and through Virginia, and about a quarter of a mile from his house, he was shot in the back six times by the police officer.

And the police officer made a number of claims about why he had done it. This was during the 2000 election, and some of you may remember Al Gore went to Howard University, there were protests and it was just an awful incident. Like a lot of people, I was just enraged and terribly affected by that. Recently the Jones family was awarded about $3 million, most of which will go to the victim's daughter. I had gotten to thinking about how does a family go on in the aftermath of that. I wanted to write about it.

But something happened, as often happens when you're writing a novel. I was writing this novel in which an African-American police officer during a stop kills a young man. But during the writing of the book, the police officer became the most compelling figure in the book.

Now the circumstances surrounding the shooting in my book are quite different from what happened in real life, but the book is really about a tragic incident in which a police officer stops someone for driving through a red light and during this stop he thinks that this person has a gun, and in fact, it turns out to be a cell phone. During this stop, because he feels threatened by what he perceives to be a weapon, he shoots and kills the young man.

As I wrote the novel, the question—the most compelling, interesting, intriguing question for me became not so much how does that family go on, even though that is part of the book, but what happens to the life of that police officer? As someone whose son had been brutalized by the police, I had a lot of attitudes about police officers. For the book, I interviewed over a dozen police officers. I rode out in cars with them and I was very lucky to meet a very, very, deep brother who was the commander of the third district in Pritchard County, where I live. He taught me and told me so much about not just the job that they do, but the contradictions of it, the difficulties, the poor training, everything. I wanted to know how a man goes on after he has essentially killed someone in a situation like that.

I had to be virtually beaten senseless into realizing that this is a story, because I didn't want to make this man the hero of my book. I had all sorts of attitudes, but my editors kept reading the manuscript and saying, "This is the most compelling character. This book has not been written." So I finally did agree with my character that he could have the book.

Susan McHenry: Oh, you were wrestling with your character a little bit?

Marita Golden: Exactly. It set me on an amazing journey that I hope will do for my readers what it did for me—surprise me, alter my perception about a lot of things, and leave me with a lot to think about. *After* is essentially a novel about forgiveness and redemption.

Susan McHenry: Well, I'm looking forward to it. I assume we have the galleys at *Black Issues Book Review* and I can't wait to read them. I will open up this conversation to our audience here; if you will, go to either one of the microphones and identify yourself and ask your question.

Female Speaker: Hi, Miss Golden. I just want to hear more about that battle that you talked about with your character. I want to hear more about the process of developing the book and where the book takes on a life and presence of its own. I want to hear how that worked for you and what the battle was like. What kind of conversations did you have?

Marita Golden: No, you don't. No you don't. [Laughter] It was horrible. Writing is a process of not just you writing the book; the book writes you. I was telling one of my classes last week that books choose us. I think that books cosmically and spiritually choose us. I worked on this book for about three years, and for the longest time I couldn't figure out why I was writing this particular book. For example, I know that one of the reasons that death plays a very important part in many of the novels that I've written is because I lost my parents at a very early age, 21 and 23, on the cusp of them being able to see the fruits of their labor with me. There is a sense in all of my novels that I have been dialoguing with my parents. I've been seeking them out. I've been saying, "I miss you. I love you," through these meditations on death.

But why was I writing this particular book? The book is about forgiveness; that's a big issue for me. I tend to be one of these A-type, very judgmental people. In writing this story in which people feel enormous guilt and enormous shame, and are asked to commit incredible acts of forgiveness, to imagine acts of forgiveness, it helped me to work through some of my own stuff.

13

So these books that we write are imaginative, but they are also nourishing our spirits in a variety of ways. The book chose me. I said, "How am I writing about a Black police officer, my goodness?" and why am I not writing it solely from just the perspective of the family, what the family has suffered? Each time I've been given a book to write, I've been assigned by God to write something that hadn't been written before. Usually, the harder you fight with a book, the more that tells you that you really do need to write it and that it has an important journey to take you on.

Don't Play in the Sun was very difficult. How in the world was I going to write about color? The light-skinned people were going to be mad with me. Dark-skinned people were going to be mad with me, and because of the type of person that I am, if I'm going to start talking about something—I'm going to talk about it. I'm going to be out front, so there was a lot of self-censorship that even after ten books, I had to battle with.

The thing that people don't realize about writing is that you have to conquer the fear every morning. The fear is there for a reason because you're doing something incredible, so of course you're supposed to be afraid, but you learn to get over it in about thirty seconds when you're writing the way you decide. I just sat there and took a knife and slit my wrist and put it over the page, because that's how deep and how true the writing had to be.

Susan McHenry: We're going to close out our evening with this last question.

Male Speaker: What has been your greatest challenge as a Black woman writer and what would be the most important advice for young aspiring Black writers?

Marita Golden: The biggest challenge I have faced was just as I said—to live in a society that is relentless, that is militant, that is creative, and that is dedicated to constantly chipping away at my sense of possibilities, and to live in that society and create an alternate space where I am the opposite of everything that society says I am. You don't do that on Monday and on Wednesday. You do it Sunday through Saturday. You do it 30 days of the month. You do it 365 days of the year. You do it all your life. So that it's the same challenge all the time. When I sat down to write my first book—who wants to read a book about a young 20-something Black woman who—my God, I had just went off to Africa, I had gotten married—the belief that I had something of value to say, and then to find that the book was read by so many people, that universities and colleges require their students to read it. Then at the age of 53, I sit down many years later and struggle with the taboo issue of colorism. So it's the same challenge in the beginning and at the end.

The advice that I would give to young Black writers, some of it's the same advice that I would give to any writer—to find some way to create that space for yourself where you're real, because there are so many factors, so many forces that are out to get you in this culture. Your family is out to get you. Your family says, "Get a job as a doctor, a lawyer. You can't make any money as a writer. So what, Terry McMillan. So what, Toni Morrison. You're not them." So you're going to have to create your own bubble, your own space, and surround yourself with like-minded people.

I tell people all the time to start a support group, a writers' group. I not only have a spiritual director; I'm a spiritual director to people and I am a member of a wisdom circle, a group of people who once a month just meet and keep each other real and cheer each other on. I think as a Black community we tend to be—actually contrary to what our mythology is—the most rugged individualists in the society. We really are the most ruggedly individuals. We have to be arm twisted into being a community with each other. That's one thing that writers need to know, that they cannot write alone. That they need to write with other people and learn from other people. Those are the challenges. But the challenge is—you learn how to take the challenges and turn them into beauty. You learn how to take blood and make it into an amazing sculpture, somehow, some way.

Susan McHenry: Thank you, Marita Golden, for your example and your wisdom, and your wonderful work.

Marita Golden: Thank you, Susan.

CHAPTER THREE

Developing a Culture of Consciousness

Haki R. Madhubuti

Using prose and poetry, Haki Madhubuti discusses his latest book, a memoir of the first 21 years of his life. He also offers reflections on his life as poet, publisher, essayist, and educator.

Madhubuti's most recent book is Yellow Black: The First Twenty-One Years of a Poet's Life. *Madhubuti weaves a memoir that draws upon his early experiences, influences, and background to describe his preparation for life as a poet, writer, publisher, editor, educator, husband, father, institution builder, and Black man. The impact of his mother's experiences, those writers who have influenced him, his life in the urban streets of Detroit, his turning points, his first literary experiences, the Vietnam War, music, the Civil Rights Movement, and the Black Arts Movement form the core of this memoir.*

Madhubuti is also the author of Tough Notes: A Healing Call for Creating Exceptional Black Men. *Over the years, he has published 28 books (some under his former name, Don L. Lee) and is one of the world's best-selling authors of poetry and nonfiction.*

When we were turned down for a charter for our proposed school, I wanted to know why we (The Institute for Positive Education) were denied this charter. The person I contacted did not know about us, or about our current school, The New Concept School, because the charter was handled in some other part of the school system. We forced him to take another look. There were only three charters left, and he asked us if we would come down to meet with him and the people who handled the charters in the Chicago Public School System, Monday. We did, my wife and I, and the Director of the Institute of Positive Education. Before that, I made sure that he received an unusual amount of telephone calls into his office. By the time we arrived on Monday morning, and as we walked into the conference room, I was ready to do battle, really ready to jump into someone's chest.

The Superintendent pulled me aside and said, "Everything is okay." He said, "Everything is fine."

He began to explain the problem. And the problem was essentially that we were not taken seriously. He didn't say that, but that was the problem.

The problem was that we were just some Black folks on the Southside of Chicago who had been in education for all these years, but we were Africans, and we had this African consciousness. That is highly unusual—for a Chicago Public School. So our question to them was, well, if it's unusual, why does it work? We have 80 to 90 percent of students leaving our school and going to the best high schools and then going to college and universities.

He said, "Okay, we don't really have to discuss this now, because we feel that you all are deserving of charter, but I have to do a walk through, and I can come through tomorrow." Which was Tuesday. We didn't really want this guy to come through the next day, but we said okay. We stayed up all night to make sure everything was fine. We were an independent school; and we had just bought a Catholic parish on the Southside of Chicago. It was literally half a block. Third World Press had the rectory, and we used the rest of it for the school.

The Superintendent came out with his associates the next day, and I told the people in the school, "Once he finishes up over there, send him over to the Third World Press." Fifteen minutes turned into two hours. This guy had never seen anything like this. Number one, you walk into a school, you don't see graffiti. You see students who are essentially engaged in the learning process, not only learning how to learn, but essentially understanding the importance of learning, so therefore, loving learning too. You see a professional staff, a professional faculty who are there because they want to be there. It's not just a job; this is a profession. It's a faculty that is essentially consulted around the development of curriculum, around the development of how we continue to move in the school, and so forth.

So when he came there, he had never witnessed that before; we have an all Black population, and as he walked around, he saw nothing but Black people running everything, everything. Us. Clean, orderly, ready for business. Serious as a first love. Why, because they're our children. They're our responsibility, and don't tell me what our children cannot do.

We are teachers, we are educators, and in the final analysis, we were like doctors, medical doctors. When you go to a medical doctor, you don't want an excuse. When you go to have your teeth fixed, you don't want an excuse. So when you send your child to us to be taught, whatever subject, there are no excuses. That child is going to come out ready to do business. That's what we've been doing for the last 35 years. This is the working vision of my wife Dr. Safisha Madhubuti (Dr. Carol D. Lee) who is a professor in the School of Education at Northwestern University.

The Superintendent had also never seen anything like Third World Press. It's one of the few Black publishing companies, well, one of only two Black publishing companies in the world that own their own buildings: Third World Press and Johnson Publishing Company. We don't rent it. We don't lease it. It is ours, in the middle of the Black community on the Southside of Chicago. We bought that property, why, because it was in the middle of the Black community on the Southside of Chicago, and the students that we receive to come into our school are not students that are picked because they have high IQ's. We want community children. We can't pick and choose. It's very important.

How did I get to this point? How did we get here? Where did this Haki Madhubuti come from? I came from where you all came from. I opened up my new memoir, *Yellow Black*, with me surrounded by pimps and ho's slamming Cadillac doors on the streets of Detroit, and Black bottom, Chicago's Westside. I was dropped into Black street culture. I became a man at twelve years old and the music of Motown, Miles Davis and Louis Armstrong kept me alive, and helped to save me, and introduced me to deep breathing, discipline and the many mysterious worlds of the trumpet.

My only point is we do not buy into excuses at all. Not any more. We don't have the time. We don't have the luxury. For me, my mentors were El-Hajj Malik El-Shabazz (Malcolm X) and Margaret and Charlie Burroughs. Margaret and Charlie Burroughs founded the DuSable Museum, the first Black museum in the country, in their home. I found them at nineteen years old. I was in the military, in the United States Army about to go crazy, and found them on the Southside of Chicago building a museum in their home.

Margaret Burroughs was and is a world-class visual artist. Charlie Burroughs, who was her husband, was raised in the USSR. He spoke Russian fluently, and he introduced me to Russian literature. He introduced me to all the Marxist literature, so when I came up against a Marxist in the 1970s, I was ready for these bad boys. I had been schooled by somebody who spoke the language.

Dudley Randall, who founded Broadside Press in Detroit, Michigan, mentored me. Hoyt W. Fuller was the Editor of *Negro Digest,* which became *Black World Magazine*, one of the major cultural vehicles of the Black Arts Movement.

Barbara Ann Sizemore. How many of you know that name? Barbara Ann Sizemore was one of the premiere educators in this country. She also mentored me. She was the one that slapped sexism out of me when I was in my 20s.

Finally, the woman who became my cultural mother for over thirty-three years was the great poet Gwendolyn Brooks. These are the people that mentored me and allowed me to become the man I am today.

How do you move from a Black boy from the lower Eastside of Detroit, Michigan and Westside Chicago, to where I'm standing on the stage here at Medgar Evers College? One of the major reasons was I learned how to read. At fourteen, my mother actually told me to go to the Detroit Public to check out a book by Richard Wright, entitled *Black Boy*. I was raised in apartheid America, so I hated myself (and I write about this in *Yellow Black)*. My mother, one of the most beautiful women in the world, I think, was in the sex trade. My father left very early.

I was born in Little Rock, Arkansas, so we moved Up South, as John Oliver Killens would say, to Detroit. My father left. He was street all the way. My father never worked for white people, always street. So my mother ended up going to a major church, one of the largest churches in Detroit, Michigan. After the pastor had finished the sermon, before she could get out the door, he was at the door greeting her, whispering in her ear, and the next week we moved into his apartment building.

Presumably, she was supposed to be the janitor, and she did that kind of work. I was ten years old; I will never forget my mother carrying garbage cans down three, four flights of stairs twice a week. Cleaning the front vestibule and so forth, but this minister would visit her twice a week on Tuesdays and Thursdays.

I'll never forget him telling her never to come back to his church, but she was his woman at least for a year and a half, until he went to the National Baptist Convention. He was running for the presidency, and somehow fell off the podium, hit his head and he died.

His wife put us out the next week and told us not to come to the funeral. My mother and another woman got an apartment together and continued to service ministers for the next four or five years. That's how they took care of their children. I can't tell you how painful it was to see your mother in the sex trade dealing with these men. What happened to me as I grew, I began to understand the power of sex and the power of beautiful women; but also how beautiful women are not protected, because my mother was not protected.

I'm not going to give the whole story, but the point is that she told me to go to Detroit Public Library and check out Richard Wright's *Black Boy*. I refused to go at first because I was ashamed of who I was. I did not want to go to a white library and ask the white librarian for a book by a Black author with the book titled, *Black Boy*; a Black author who was being critical of white America, but I did. I went to the Detroit Public Library, found the book on the shelf, put the book to my chest, walked to an unpeopled section of the library, and sat down and began to read. For the first time in my life, at fourteen years old, six foot one, 131 pounds, looking like a walking skeleton, I was reading literature that was not an insult to my own personhood.

I was reading words, sentences, and paragraphs essentially that talked about me. Richard Wright's *Black Boy* was essentially about a young, Black boy who was highly intelligent, which is not unusual for us; he wanted to be a writer, and the story is what he went through in order to achieve his dream.

I wasn't really writing at that time. I was just writing little poems here and there, just the introspections of a young boy growing up in deep, deep pain. But Richard Wright's nonfiction told me; he told me, it was very clear that I could become a writer. This was what Richard Wright did for me. I checked the book out, took it home and read it in less than 24 hours. I gave the book to my mother to read and the next day, went back to the library and checked out everything Richard Wright had published.

That gave me an escape to some saneness. We grew up beneath poverty. Is there a word for that? Sub-poverty? I was telling a brother a little earlier, I didn't get my first new suit until my mother's funeral at sixteen years old. I grew up wearing second-hand everything. You don't hear Negroes wearing second-hand socks, second-hand underwear, second-hand everything. The Salvation Army was like my second home.

I endured, but it really had disastrous effects on my sister. My sister is one and a half years younger than I, and I had to get permission from her to publish *Yellow Black*. My sister had her first child at fourteen, her second child at sixteen, and her third child at eighteen. By the time she was twenty-seven, she had six children, and never married—there were four different fathers. None of these men ever helped.

I'm saying that we all have our horror stories. The key is now how do you eclipse these horror stories? How do you use these horror stories? How do you develop all these horror stories and move toward what we call liberation narratives? Liberation narratives. I'm tired of booty call. I am tired of it, but the liberation narratives have got to find the eyes and the ears and the mind of our young people. But in order for them to find it, in many cases the teachers have to be aware of these liberation narratives.

The teachers have to be bold enough and strong enough to bring liberation narratives into the classrooms.

This is what I was saying earlier. We are not going to win this war, and you can quote me on this; we are not going to win this war unless we get the right material into grade schools and high schools. We need to spend quality time with our children, especially the men. I talk about this all the time. The real problem with brothers is that we can rap for days, but if you want to rap and you want to have an audience, where is the best audience than these schools on a daily basis?

But you cannot get into a classroom unless you are credentialed. In order to be credentialed, you have to go through Medgar Evers or some other college or university, which requires something that most brothers do not have: discipline. Discipline. To stick to it, and to say, "This is what I'm going to do. This is my mission. This is my five-year goal. This is my ten-year goal."

If you are Black in America, you've had it difficult. Everybody has a horror story, but I'm tired of ignorant people telling me how ignorant other people are. We need to do more to move toward a sense of ownership; we have to understand who we are as a people and our own history, our own culture; we have to understand how we have gotten here.

Very little has changed. White world supremacy actually is a political system. It's a political system that works worldwide, and it's effective. How else could less than nine percent of the world's population run the world? How else?

So for me the literature was critical, because I didn't know anything about myself. For us to begin to move toward levels of ownership, first and foremost, you have to own yourself. That means culturally, economically, socially. It is ownership that is critical. It's very important. You have to layer your own life with your own knowledge, first and foremost. Why is this?

Essentially, if you have a body of knowledge behind you, in front of you, beside you, you will understand how critical this is, and any people who are in control of their own cultural imperatives will understand that. Very seldom do you hear white people calling each other, "You white so-and-so. You white B." You look at culture-to-culture, whether it's Irish, the Polish, Jewish, the Italian in Chicago; they have their stuff pretty much together.

When I say ownership, what does that mean? I'm a vegan. If it runs from me, I'm not going to eat it. If I have to chase it, it's not going to get cooked. All right, I know I'm different. I practice yoga. I know I'm different, all right? I'm a cyclist; I ride bikes and stuff like that. I spent a certain amount of time in India. I spent a whole lot of time in Africa. I'm saying I went to India basically because I was looking to try to really understand the fundamentals of yoga, and this special diet I was on, but I didn't become Indian. I'm still an African. Do you see my point? Once you are layered in yourself, you can go anywhere, touch anybody else's knowledge, gain from that knowledge and keep on going. Then, the wise of us will incorporate that knowledge within the context of what we're teaching, or what we feel is in the best interest of our people.

Coming up as a kid, I really didn't understand this until my mother—my mother use to do day work—took us to Dearborn, Michigan. The men who actually founded and were building the automobile industry in Detroit, Michigan populated Dearborn. So we were on the bus going to Dearborn, Michigan. Now in Detroit, you saw a five-and-dime store, a Woolworth store, the liquor stores, and the barbershops. As soon as you hit Dearborn, Michigan, you see green. If you were passing the stores, they were craft shops and hobby shops.

So right there it hit me. I'm ten, eleven years old and, what's this? This is another world.

We had gotten to the mansion that my mother was cleaning up that day. The family was out of town, but the mansion was as large as this whole damn auditorium right here. As my mother was cleaning up, we were walking through and I walked into a child's room. I knew it was a child's room. In that room, on the table there was some wood and some paper. As I walked over to it, I saw that it was a model airplane. Now understand I had just turned ten, eleven years old and my mother had just bought me an airplane for my birthday, but it was a blue plastic airplane, with a blue plastic string, propellers and wheels that I rolled along the linoleum. You know what linoleum is? I guess some of you may know. I was happy to get that plastic airplane, but out there in that upper white middle class home, and walking into that child's room, seeing that model airplane, it became very clear to me that that child may have been my age. I didn't know. But it was very clear to me that that child would put that plane together learning mathematics and science, and most certainly could read. Essentially, the whole idea of a work ethic in putting the plane together was made clear. And guess what? After he or she put the plane together, they would take the plane outside and it would fly. That's what planes do.

It was very clear to me that there were two types of consciousness being developed in America. In the Black community, consumerism, you buy it and hope it works. In the white community, in the upper class, white community, you buy the toy; it's a working toy; you put it together, so you use it neck up rather than neck down.

Essentially, what's happened is that you build upon that experience of putting that plane together, and soon you start running the companies and people are working for you. Whereas for us, the consumerism, we buy what they make, we come through Medgar Evers, or some other kind of school, and hope we can get a job some place. We don't even think about ownership. Don't think about, "Can I run this myself? Can I do a better job? How can I pull together the money to do this?"

We're not thinking that way, and that starts, brothers and sisters, very early. At two and a half years old, that's when you start to think about yourself in the context of a world that you control yourself.

Where are these cultural families? These cultural families are very important. Here we are at Medgar Evers and we're talking about writing, so you have to have a writing family. You have to have other men and women who are engaged in the same type of pursuit of excellence in terms of your writing that you can feed stuff off of, because there is nothing as lonely as a writer. At least a musician occasionally comes together with other musicians, but writing, you're by yourself most times.

There is very little collective writing going on, so you're on your own trying to create the poem; you're trying to create the short story; you're trying to create the novel, the novella—whatever the case may be.

This is why conferences like this are critical and very important. We do this every year ourselves at Chicago State, the third weekend in October, the annual Gwendolyn Brooks Conference. This is a writing family.

During late 1960s, I worked with and was one of the founding members of the Organization of Black American Culture Writers Workshop, which was lead by the late great editor, educator, public intellectual and activist, Hoyt W. Fuller. Finding a

26

mentor is critical for young people. There are men and women out here who you do not even know, who actually love you, who actually care for you. It's your responsibility to try to find those persons. They're here at Medgar Evers, they're at most schools, but you need to try to find those persons and try to share your work with them. These writing families are very, very important.

I think now is a good time to share a poem. It's called "A Poet's Call."

It has always been easy

to get to my heart.

there is no other way of stating it.

the best poets are lovers,

are receptacles for pain, joy, injustice

and the innocent smiles of children.

we trust too early and easily.

we read potential in the countless faces of evil.

we carry many, many wounds

we are often crippled, yet some heal quickly

only to open their hearts to stories our

children can see through.

the right words can send us on unlimited journeys.

the hurt in children's eyes release fury

in our souls and fists.

Black girls' mistreated hair brings tears.

I do not wish it to always be this way

to care too much can damage one's spirit, yet,

the secret to the longevity of significant poets is:

we never give up on love, poetry and

the smiles of the young.

(Madhubuti xiii)

The first question for all of us, and most certainly for young people is, "Who am I?" Who am I? I can walk into your home and not know you, and tell you within fifteen minutes who you are, because your home essentially is the best definer of who you are. As soon as I walk into your home I'm going to see if it's clean. That's the first thing. As I walk into the living room, I'm going to look at your walls and see what kinds of pictures, photographs, and paintings occupy your home. Do all those photographs and paintings reflect you? It's significant.

Then I'm going to your bookshelf, if you have a bookshelf, and see what kind of books you're reading. Then I'm going over to your music section, look at the CDs, old school albums. See who you're listening to, see what kind of liberation music you're listening to. Then I'm going over to the DVDs and VCRs, and especially look at the ones that are wrapped up in the brown paper bags, and see what you're looking at.

But to really see where a family is, you go into the children's room. See what's on their walls. Darth Vader, Mickey Mouse, Donald Duck. See why confusion reigns.

It starts with the children. This is why we tell our parents that your home has to become a mini-learning institution. What we're sharing with your children, teaching your children each and every day here at our schools, it has to be duplicated at home. That child cannot come here for five, six, seven, eight hours and go home to deep confusion and contradictions. Our schools open up at seven o'clock and go till six or seven o'clock and if children go home and get the exact opposite information, we will undoubtedly fail. It's not going to work, and we will find out what's happening within the first few weeks what is going on.

This question of, "Who am I?" If it's answered with a historical, political, economic, social and cultural context by Black people or people of African ancestry, also known as African-Americans, and drilled in often, there will be less confusion about black identity, purpose, potential and one's place in a highly nationalistic and multi-cultural world.

I've studied this question for over forty years. Blackness or one's Africanness when interpreted by persons without a serious cultural education is generally limited to one's personal struggle with day-to-day survival. This tends to be anti what one is struggling against. Therefore, to be Black, too often in the West, is to be a victim, and as such, one is always responding to anti-Black racism, In effect, white supremacy. So a person's Blackness or color is very seldom a positive affirmation of a whole self.

In America it is mostly limited to negative generalities of Black people. It's popular and consumer culture that guides most of us. This includes a wide variety of things from the food we eat, the religion we practice, the politics we espouse, to the clothes we wear, as well as our dance music, hair, language, and so forth. Black popular culture is portrayed through current popular Black television shows, radio shows, rap, and so forth, in addition to certain businesses. The businesses that populate the Black community that we own are, for the most part, beauty shops, barbershops, bars, taverns, liquor stores, and a thriving underground economy—but the major business of the Black community is the Black church.

The other major business in the Black community is the undertaker. The Black undertakers get off scot-free. They do that stuff after you die. Nobody is coming after them for money. They just bury you. On the other hand, the Black church is not only a business; now it's also become a very political organization.

We do not own the Black community as it stands now. Brothers out on the corners talking about how bad they are, and this is my turf, etc., etc. They're paying rent. We have to understand that just because you are Black, does not mean you understand what Blackness is. When we're talking about Blackness, we're not only just talking about color; we're talking about culture and consciousness. So your culture gives you a sense of who you are. It's a larger context. From your culture comes the consciousness. Just because you are Black does not mean that you are the noun Black with a capital B. You actually may be a Negro.

It is your responsibility if you are a thinking individual, if you are an intellectual, to think critically. If I'm incorrect, if I'm wrong, you tell me I'm wrong, or incorrect, or you question what I say.

It is our responsibility to call them out. Barack Obama is now a Senator from Illinois, who I used to call on the telephone, and we'd come and sit down, have lunch together and talk together. If I can't get in touch with him now, I want to know what the problem is. I want to know why you've taken corporate jets. What is the problem? You move from a State Senator, to become a Senator on a national level; you're not taking regular planes anymore. You're taking corporate jets. If you've taken a corporate jet, somebody is sitting next to you, whispering into your ear. Now you are a multi-millionaire because now people are buying your book, and now you have a two, three book deal with a major publisher, and your wife gets to do a children's book. You're a multi-millionaire now. Why can't I and others get in touch with you anymore?

What has changed? I'm going to tell you what's changed. Money has changed. Your whole relationship with other people, white people in position of power and influence, that has changed, whereas before you were part of the community, walking through the community every day; we could touch you and everything else. [Please note: Since the time this lecture was presented in 2006, Senator Barack Obama has now emerged as a serious candidate for the Democratic nomination for President of the United States. I whole heartedly and enthusiastically support and encourage his candidacy. Also note that shortly after the corporate jet incident, Obama ceased his actions in that regard and has since co-sponsored new ethical legislation for better oversight of individual Congressional leaders.]

Money talks, but I'm saying essentially what we need, and what we have to understand is that what Black people need are people who are serious. The most serious thing we have to be concerned about is our children. Our children. I could have been famous as Don L. Lee. I have no doubt about that whatsoever. I could have been famous as Don L. Lee, but that is not the important thing. What is important is how do we move toward authenticity? So changing my name to Haki Madhubuti, Madhubuti nobody can even pronounce half the time, which comes from the Kiswahili language spoken I East Africa. I didn't pick my own name. Haki means just or justice. Madhubuti means precise, accurate, dependable. I think it's an accurate name. So you try to live up to it. Just because you make a little bit of money does not remove you from your community, does not take you away from doing that which is right, just and correct.

We have to be constructively critical of Black leadership. At the same time, we have to be about bettering ourselves. I hope I will be better next year, if I come back in New York than I was this year. You have to keep moving, keep developing. Keep developing everywhere you are, and don't tell people what you can't do. Don't let anybody tell you what you can't do. The key to our success always is how we layer and use knowledge about ourselves, others and the world.

This is what I learned from Malcolm. A lot of people thought that Malcolm was radical, that Malcolm was a militant, but Malcolm X was actually just sane. We were the ones that were backwards. It's very clear to me that, essentially, we always have to stay on this learning curve. Let me bring this down a little bit.

The artist is able to see what our tomorrows must be like. Why is it that forty million Black people in America are going through what we're going through everyday. It doesn't make any sense. The only reason this can happen is because we are unconscious. Let's get back to where I started: Black, the color, the culture and consciousness. I say that part of the answer to this; I think a supreme part of the answer is art. I'll just end with this piece here, because art is very important. It's critical. I'm going to need your help on this. "Art."

> Art is fundamental instruction and food for a
> people's soul as they translate the many languages

31

and acts of becoming, often telling them in no uncertain terms that all humans are not pure or perfect. However, the children of all cultures inherit their creators' capacity to originate from the bone of their imaginations, the closest manifestations of purity, perfection and beauty. Art at its best encourages us to walk on water, dance on top of trees, and skip from star to star without being able to swim, keep a beat or fly. A child's "on fire" imagination is the one universal prerequisite for becoming an artist.

Magnify your children's minds with art,

jumpstart their questions with art,

introduce your children to the cultures of the world through art,

energize their young feet, spirits and souls with art,

infuse the values important to civil culture via art.

keep them curious, political and creative with art. speak and define the universal language of beauty with art,

learn to appreciate peace with art,

approach the cultures of others through their art,

introduce the spiritual paths of other people through their art,

keep young people in school, off drugs

and out of prison with art,

keep their young minds running, jumping

and excited with art.

examine the nurturing moments of love,

peace and connecting differences with art.

Art allows and encourages the love of self and others. The best artists are not mass murderers, criminals or child molesters; they are in the beauty and creation business. Art is elemental to intelligence, working democracy, freedom, equality and justice. Art, if used wisely and widely, early and often, is an answer and a question. It is the cultural lake that the indigenous rivers of dance, music, local images and voices flow. Art is the waterfall of life, reflecting the untimely and unique soul of a people. Art is the drumbeat of good and great hearts forever seeking peace and a grand future for all enlightened peoples. For these are the people the world over who lovingly proclaim, "give the artist some." Kind words, financial support, yeses from your heart, knowing intuitively that there will be creative reciprocity in all that they give us. Why? Because fundamentally, art inspires, informs, directs, generates hope and challenges the receiver to respond. Finally, and this is consequential, the quality of the art determines the quality of the responses.

(Madhubuti 129-131)

Thank you very much. [Applause] I'd be glad to entertain any questions you may have at this time.

Female speaker: That was a great lecture. Thank you. My name is Deborah. I spoke at one of the other panel sessions. I came in from Denver, Colorado. I just want to add to your story about the model airplane, a real story of success. My father put us in model airplane contests and all types of things. You gave a good example of what it takes to put a model airplane together. He did all of that.

To be the only Black family at a model airplane contest is something probably no one but we can comprehend, but I just want to say the success of that, even though it came from what you would call maybe a white concept for a Black family, produced a pilot. One of my brothers builds and flies gliders out in California. It got me on an airplane today to come here, and that airplane was co-piloted by a Black man by the name of Luther. Even though it is a white concept, it's important. It's necessary; the discipline is there and in no way do we feel we have to compromise our Blackness to do that. So I just want to encourage you on and everyone else. I thank you for your thoughts.

Haki Madhubuti: Thank you. [Applause] Thank you very much. Just to add to what she said, our middle boy, and I really didn't talk about my children, but my middle boy is a civil engineer. He started building bridges with toothpicks; then he moved to building bridges with straws. Now he is a civil engineer.

Male Speaker: I have a question for you. I was listening to your talk, and in listening to it, it reminded me of things that I had heard, and in fact had said, forty years ago.

Back then it was Nation Time, and Black is Beautiful. Everybody wore 'froes because we were all Afrocentric at that time. My question to you—I have my own thoughts on this, but I'd like to hear your thoughts on where we are now relative to where we were forty years ago. Have we made progress? Have we not made progress? What is the continuum that we are embracing today?

Haki Madhubuti: This is an unfinished agenda. I think that now you have a very large, Black middle class community that is one paycheck away from impoverishment. For the first time in our history we have more educated Black men and women with specific skills, but who are very unconscious. We have many men and women who have graduated from research one universities, Black men and women—who come out and don't know anything about themselves. They get out there in the job market and get

34

slapped, and then wonder why they're getting slapped. Some have no concept, no political concept or cultural concept of themselves as people of African ancestry in this country.

This is a very serious question though, and I've had to deal with this. You have to be guerilla warriors. What a guerilla warrior is, is a woman or a man who may be working for a Fortune 1000, Fortune 500 company, who understands that he or she is in this position because Affirmative Action exists. Number two, they are skilled and they wouldn't be there unless they were skilled. The fallacy about Affirmative Action is this: If you are able to attend or be employed at a research one university, it doesn't matter whether or not Affirmative Action helped you to get that position; Affirmative Action will not help you to keep it. You must work to retain your position.

My point is, as a guerilla warrior you may work in a company and you will look around and you may say, "Well, I'm the only one here." That is a problem. What you should think as a guerilla warrior is, "how can I work to get other people who look like me up in here?" Once that happens, you may get with these same people who are with you now, saying, "Look, how we can start our own company?"

Fundamentally, we are not going to gain ground unless we start owning something, begin to run something, begin to essentially own. What buildings do we own in Downtown Manhattan? None. That's just part of it.

You're not going to hear from me ever backing up on this question around race. I'm just not going to do it. I'm 64 years old. I've been around here long enough, endured enough, and just because we have a book on the *New York Times* Bestseller list—this is the first time a Black publishing company ever hit the *New York Times* Bestseller list—don't anywhere in your mind think that's going to change us at Third World Press, or me, Haki Madhubuti. Let me just sum this up. Our future is in our hands, and why do I say that, because I understand history. My teacher was Chancellor

Williams. My teachers were John Henrik Clarke, Yosef ben-Jochannan, W.E.B. DuBois, Paul Robeson, Carter G. Woodson, and Lerone Bennett; so I understand that long continuum, that whole long line of history. We are in a position, actually of empowerment, but we don't use what we have. There is no excuse for ignorance in the Black community when you live in a nation with a free library system. It doesn't make any sense at all. I do not take excuses from students. We don't take excuses from students. If I'm a mentor, if I'm a father, when you come through me, you are going to work. That is what I'm saying, we are turning out talented young people everyday at our schools. That is why my wife and I put so much time and energy into developing these schools. They are more important than our own personal careers. We have to build these warriors to come out here and continue to fight, and recognize that wherever you live, that's the Black community. Therefore, we have to move toward ownership at every single level. Remember, we're not going anywhere. America was built on the backs of our ancestors, enslaved Africans, who worked from sun-up to sun-down and who were given bad food and the rags on their backs. Our ancestors built this country and it owes us a great deal.

Why is that important? Because out of all the Black people in the world, we are the most educated. We have the most potential and access. We have access to education, to clean water, to food, housing, clothing and to challenging employment and opportunities. The great majority of people in the world go to sleep every night hungry. That's why I'm on this.

Female Speaker: Thank you for the work of Third World Press over the years. It's really been an inspiration. It's encouraging to writers to know that you are there. I wanted to ask you about the press, because we're here this weekend as writers and I think it's important that we discuss the access to materials.

I was reading last night about how many of our books are now out of print. We talk about the schools. I was a teacher, as well. I know how often we're looking to buy books to take them into the schools, and how few opportunities there are for writers, for young people even, to make sure that once their books are written, that they will reach the communities. Could you talk about publishing for a moment and that dynamic of distribution?

Haki Madhubuti: Sure. Let me just say this first. I told Dr. Brenda Greene that if she wanted to pull together the papers from the conference, to edit these papers, write an introduction, and put them into context that we would be glad to publish them. We will do that. So I made that commitment.

The real problem in publishing, most certainly in Black publishing is that there are not enough of us and too little capital to work with. The other significant publisher—now Johnson Publishing, the oldest of the Black publishers, publishes primarily Lerone Bennett Jr. in terms of books. The other publishers are Black Classic Press out of Baltimore, Paul Coates; African World Press, Kassahun Checole; and Just Us Books, Wade and Cheryl Hudson, which is a children's book company out of New Jersey. Amber Books, Tony Rose, out of Phoenix is another.

There are only about five or six serious publishers who publish multiple copies, not a single author. We receive about 30 manuscripts a day. There is no way in the world that we can go through all that material. Two things. One, I think that collectives should form groups to publish. Two, you are talking about out-of-print material? There is a lot of material in the public domain, which means essentially, it can be published.

We're looking at a lot of material, but it takes a lot of time. What I'm interested is reading materials that are going to allow us to move to the next level in terms of our development.

We also have the Third World Press Foundation. This foundation is charged with helping to building libraries in public schools; building libraries in children's and women's shelters; and building libraries in the prison systems across this country. Third World Press Foundation is charged with publishing literary writers.

Out of our Foundation we're going to publish the poets and the literary fiction writers. We couldn't do it with the regular press, because it is not profitable, but we're going to do it now with the Foundation. Go to our website at www.thirdworldpressinc.com and you can see what we are doing.

Female Speaker: Earlier you said that you felt that beautiful women were unprotected. What did you mean by that, and who protects them, and how?

Haki Madhubuti: I, as a father, have to protect my children, my daughters. As long as they're my daughters, they are under my protection. I don't care if they are adults. They're still under my protection. So I'm saying if some Negro approaches my daughters in the wrong way; if they even think about putting their hands on them, they have to come through me. My mother wasn't protected. My mother was a beautiful woman. At 17 she was on the streets. She was not protected; that's what I mean.

That's why families are so important. I'm talking about my daughters now, but I'm talking about my sons also, because on a certain level they had to be protected until they are able to deal with it themselves, and even when they become adults, I'm still their father.

Beautiful women—this world, this country is controlled and run by white men. Black men are in a serious position because of a lack of power, one of the real problems in the Black community we don't talk about. I do, however, write about it in *Tough Notes*, and I wrote about it in *Black Men* and in *Claiming Earth*. We don't talk about rape in the Black community. Rape exists because too many men are unconscious; they are angry and they are powerless. They hate most people. They hate themselves, and also hate the women that they are raping. That's not an excuse, but a fact.

So it is my responsibility, and other conscious men's responsibility to fight against rape. I saw what happened to my mother. I couldn't do anything about it. I was a young teenager. I will never forget this; I write about this in the book; my stepfather had come home and my mother was high, and he started beating her up for whatever the reason. So I grabbed a butcher knife and came at him. I pulled him off of her and told him that he will not see tomorrow if he ever puts his hands on her again. I said, "I will kill you after you are dead." I remember, and he never hit her again, but it was too late. She was gone. He was definitely gone.

That's my point. In this country sexism is out of order. Not only here, I read about six papers a day, and about four or five magazines a week. You still see in other parts of the world, so-called honor killings going on. In India this week, a doctor was locked up for telling the woman and the husband the gender of their child, because in India if a child is a girl, there is a great possibility that she will be aborted. There is a law against telling the gender of the child.

There are a couple of things just totally out-of-whack in terms of what women have to go through in order to become whole people. That's why I write about this and other critical matters. That's why many of my books speak directly to men on issues concerning women, self discipline, building consciousness and empowerment, and you know what? That's all right. Thank you.

Works Cited
Madhubuti, Haki R. *ToughNotes: A Healing Call For Creating Exceptional Black Men*. Chicago, Third World Press, 2002.

CHAPTER FOUR

HISTORY AS NARRATIVE

Moderator: Adam McKible
Panelists: Herb Boyd, Valerie Boyd,
and Christopher John Farley

This panel explores an important part of the African American experience in the Americas. We were often portrayed as a people without a history. Yet, it was Black writers, from the slave narratives to the early poet, novelist and memoirists, who bore witness and told, against all odds, the story of a people. They dealt with perceptions of Black people in society and portrayed the complexity of the racial history of Black people and the ways that historical narrative shaped the past and future.

Adam McKible: In what ways do historical narratives portray the racial history of this nation? How do historical narratives help us to reclaim our past and shape our future?

Herb Boyd: When I heard about being a participant on this particular panel, the first question that came to mind was one of definition and how to define exactly what we are talking about.

About five years ago, for about five years, I taught a course at New York University called Creative Nonfiction. When I was asked to be on this panel, I thought, "Oh, this sounds like creative nonfiction again." In teaching that course, I struggled for definition, to find out exactly what was it all about, because it was absolutely a new genre, a new field, a new discipline. However, with narrative as history, I thought maybe another working definition might be gained, historical fiction. I was in a bookstore recently and there was this article, *The Best Historical Fiction*, which listed fifty books. Of course, what crossed my mind was out of the fifty books, how many of them were Black? One was. What do you think it was? *Roots*. Exactly. *Roots*. And when you think about *Roots*, then, of course, there is the whole fiction and fact confluence again. What is absolutely factual, and then what is fictional?

I think Alex Haley came up with an answer. He said, "Factional." You have to bleed the two things together. If you say then that *Roots* is an exemplary text on the topic for the discussion we'll have this afternoon, that of course, brings to mind works going back in African-American history like William Wells Brown's book, *Clotel, The President's Daughter*, written in the 1850s. It was considered one of the first black novels until Skip (Henry Louis) Gates Jr. came along with Harriet Wilson's, *Our Nig*, which supplanted it.

I think of Barbara Chase-Riboud and the books that she's done, particularly, *The President's Daughter*, which of course is a continuation of what William Wells Brown had done earlier looking at the relationship between Thomas Jefferson and Sally

42

Hemings. Barbara came out with another book called *Sally Hemings*, and of course, I think to a large degree that falls within the definition of historical fiction.

Currently I'm reading a book by Kevin Baker called *Strivers Row*. Here again, you have a meditation on history, where Harlem becomes almost like a character in the book. You look at it historically, so you say how far back do you have to go before its historical fiction. Fifty years ago? One hundred years ago? Kevin is writing in a contemporary way, but he's reflecting or meditating on Harlem in the 1940s. His principal character is Malcolm X. Only he's calling him Malcolm Little until he goes through the other incarnations of Detroit Red, Satan, Malcolm X, and El-Hajj Malik El-Shabazz. For the most part he's focusing on 1943. Thus far I'm about half way through the book and I think some of us "Malcolmites" are going to be a little bit upset with some of the characterization. Is it consistent with what we understand to be the character and integrity of one Malcolm X or Malcolm Little?

At the same time, I'm reminded of William Styron's book, *The Confessions of Nat Turner*, which is another so-called meditation on history. It was an abysmal, absolute failure on his part. So much so that ten Black writers back in 1968-69 felt compelled to respond to Styron because, for the most part, he'd taken the confessions of Nat Turner and did his own particular getting inside of Nat Turner's head, and produced a kind of a psychoanalytical probe of the man and what might have been his reaction to a particular set of circumstances. So that was an absolute failure, though he was in concert with James Baldwin for a good part of the time in Connecticut while he wrote that book.

David Durham has a book called *A Pride of Carthage*, where he looks at the life of Hannibal. My first concern was let me get into this book and see how far along will we read before we find out what color is Hannibal, because we have had other takes on Hannibal's life, and for the most part, all of the white historians, novelists, what have you, depicted Hannibal as being white. What David does is flip the script completely here, and present Hannibal as a black man. I'm about 75 pages into the book, and I am pleased to know that he had that kind of perspective on it.

If you go back and look at Dumas, Pushkin, and look at some of the other writers in the Third World, and how they've dealt with the question of historical fiction, there's been a marvelous production of material. Perhaps in this discussion, not only can we move to a definition, but also begin to cite some of the current contemporary books that reflect and characterize what we might call historical fiction.

Valerie Boyd: Herb Boyd was talking about historical fiction, and I think that's an important place to start the conversation, but I'd like to move us to also talk about nonfiction. Research based nonfiction and the importance, the imperative of narrative in telling our true historical stories. My book, *Wrapped in Rainbows: The Life of Zora Neale Hurston* is not fiction. It is a biography. It is non-fiction. I don't make up any quotes. I don't make up any scenarios. It's based on four and a half years of research, where I really explored Hurston's life. I read and have copies of more than 600 letters that she wrote to friends and acquaintances, like Langston Hughes, Richard Wright, Marita Bonner and other writers from the Harlem Renaissance era.

This is a book of nonfiction, but using Herb's term, creative nonfiction, it's also written, or I attempted to write it in a way that was engaging. I attempted to use the tools of the novelist, such as dialogue, plot and character development. I attempted to use those tools to make it an engaging narrative. For me that's an important thing for us to talk about and to think about as we think about telling our true histories, our true stories, but telling them in a way that makes these books accessible to a wide range of readers.

I think that we as writers—and I'm assuming that a lot of you in the audience are writers, or aspiring writers—have a responsibility to tell our histories and to tell them in a way that makes people want to read them. We don't have to write dry, academic books in telling our histories. I think it's possible, and in

44

fact, necessary for us to write our own histories in ways that engage a wide range of readers. We can use the tools of the novelist to do that. I used Langston Hughes and Zora Neale Hurston's letters to create a whole conversation between them when they were arguing about a play they wrote together called *Mule Bone*. I don't make up any dialogue, but I quote from their letters, and present it in a way that it feels like, or my goal was that it would feel like you were actually right there in the middle of their argument, but nothing is made up. It's based on the research.

I really would encourage us to do more of that kind of writing. Research based nonfiction. If you are a writer and you feel that you have talent as a writer, our history is an untapped area of exploration, which you can explore with historical fiction as Herb was talking about, where you find a story from our past, find a story from our history, and embellish on it and just have the freedom to write about it as fiction; or you can approach it as I did with Zora Neale Hurston's story and really do the research. Really find out the truth of what happened, and then use your writing skills, your skills as a storyteller, to write that kind of historical nonfiction in a way that engages.

I know high school students and college students are reading my biography of Zora Neale Hurston because I purposely wrote it in a way that it would be accessible. That doesn't undermine the scholarship of it. I have pages and pages of end notes, so if people want to just read it as a story and never check the end notes, they can just read it as a story that engages, but if they want to know where I got any piece of information from, there is a note on almost every fact that I present here, because they are all facts, and they are all research.

I'd like for us to talk about that a little bit more in the question and answer portion of this discussion, but I just really wanted to put a plug in for research-based nonfiction. Anything that you're interested in, you can become an expert on it by doing enough research, and then using your skills as a storyteller to write about it in a way that will pull readers in. That will make readers just fly through the pages.

One of my challenges when I was writing this book was how do I begin to tell this story. I had done four and a half years of research on Zora Neale Hurston's life. I have visited archives all around the country. Everything that was in her possession at the time of her death is at the University of Florida in Gainesville. I spent several weeks there. A lot of her Harlem Renaissance correspondence with Langston Hughes and others is at Howard University in D.C., so I spent weeks there. Several of her original manuscripts are at Yale including the original manuscript for *Their Eyes Were Watching God*, handwritten.

It was amazing to pick up that manuscript. My hands were shaking. Zora Neale Hurston wrote in longhand, in pencil, and you can see her handwriting slightly sloping. With *Their Eyes Were Watching God*, you see where she began to write and she didn't like the way it was starting, so she crossed out the first two lines, flipped the page over and started again. Then it just flows from there. She said the novel was dammed up in her, and in fact, it feels like that when you read the original manuscript. She wrote it in six weeks in Haiti. As you all know, Zora Neale Hurston was also a folklorist and anthropologist, so a lot of her anthropological research is at the Library of Congress in D.C., so I spent weeks there.

Again, nonfiction as well as historical fiction, I think are both valid kinds of endeavors for us with narrative and with story telling as the key ingredient in both cases.

Christopher John Farley: I've read *Wrapped in Rainbows*. It really is a terrific book. I can't recommend it more highly. By the way, since we're at Medgar Evers College, there will be a quiz on this afterwards, so get your number two pencils out. [Laughter] I think the point that I'm making is people sometimes think that history is something fixed like mathematics. That it's there set in stone, but history really is something more like figure skating judging, where it's very subjective and the results that are actually announced may not match with what you are seeing before your own eyes.

We all get a sense of the first draft of history with some recent history. We've read the papers. We've seen what's happening in Iraq and Afghanistan with elections. Right before our eyes we've seen it all pass by. We've lived history. Then the results, the things that we see recorded may not match up to what we actually thought we observed. If that can happen with an event that happened a day ago, or last week, or a year ago, just imagine what happens with history when it's ten years ago, or twenty, or thirty, or forty, or four hundred years ago. Things really get changed. They get altered. They get filtered through other people.

One thing that has always been particularly disturbing to me is that we usually don't get to tell our own history. That's one reason I wrote, *Before the Legend: The Rise of Bob Marley*.

For a long time, I worked as a music critic at *Time* magazine. I'm now an editor at the *Wall Street Journal*, but one thing that I always noted is that although Black people were the engines of much of popular music in the US—the inventors of Rock and the Blues, R&B—most of the biographies written about the greatest Black artists, weren't written by African Americans. They were written by other people who had other interpretations about what was going on. That colors the interpretation of history. Things get left out.

That's precisely what I found when I did my research for my book. Things that were commonly accepted as facts, and were in all the encyclopedias, websites and books about Bob Marley, I found to be false, to have not been researched properly; to not have matched up to what I found by going to Jamaica, talking to people, going to their homes, going into the hills and meeting people who knew Bob Marley way back when, and getting the real story, getting documents that proved certain facts actually happened.

I'll give you one example. One of the most famous things about Bob Marley is that he is biracial, that his father is an English captain and his mother is Black. Even his family tells this story. But I found in doing the research and through finding documents that that wasn't true. His father wasn't white. His father was actually a man of color who was passing as white according to the documents, and a lot of things that people thought about him weren't true. For instance, he wasn't a captain. He was actually discharged as a private. He wasn't British; he was actually Jamaican. He wasn't in his 40s when he married Bob Marley's mother who was a teenager then. He was actually in his 60s.

Things like that that we accept because they have been written in a lot of books, but aren't necessarily true when we check them out ourselves. The only way to rewrite history is for us to write it ourselves, because the history that we see often isn't the right history.

Adam McKible: My job is just to keep the conversation rolling, so let me just phrase my questions based on some of the things that I heard. I'll start with Valerie. I was wondering how the idea of creative nonfiction, research driven creative nonfiction differs from historical fiction? Herb, when you were talking about this list of the fifty greatest historical novels, and only *Roots* was mentioned, I wanted to ask, "What about Toni Morrison's *Beloved*?" She won a Nobel Prize. I wanted to mention Ishmael Reed, who is speaking later, wrote *Mumbo Jumbo*, which is such a great representation of the Harlem Renaissance. I also mention *Flight To Canada*, for the way it treats slave narratives and runaway slaves.

How do you think that historical fiction differs from historical nonfiction? Do we get at different truths through these kinds of approaches?

Valerie Boyd: I think they differ only in that one is fiction and one is nonfiction. In historical fiction, you are free, as Toni Morrison was in *Beloved*, to find a story like she found in the story of Margaret Garner. Then she created characters who may or may not have existed just by diving into her imagination, and using this historical truth, or this historical fact as a jumping board for her imagination.

48

With research based nonfiction, you are writing truth. Things have to be documented, so you can't just dive into your imagination and make up characters. I didn't make up characters who interacted with Zora Neale Hurston. I tell the truth about her life, and I'm glad that Chris said what he said about finding so-called facts in your research that prove not to be true. I had the same experience in writing about Zora Neale Hurston. There are all kinds of things that we accept about her mythology that I found not to be true.

For instance, there is the whole legend of Zora Neale Hurston dying poor, penniless and alone in Florida. It's true that she didn't have a lot of money at the end of her life, but Zora Neale Hurston never made a lot of money in her lifetime. The largest royalty she ever made from any of her books was $943. The largest advance she ever made from any of her books was $500, while white writers were routinely getting $5,000 advances.

Her story was not a rags-to-riches-to-rags story. She never had the riches, but she was committed to making her living as a writer, even when it didn't pay well. At the end of her life, when she died in 1960, she didn't have a lot of money, but she was not alone. She was part of a community in Fort Pierce, Florida.

I went to Fort Pierce and I interviewed a half dozen people who knew her. She was a substitute teacher at the high school. I've interviewed many of her former students. She was a part of a community. She had a beautiful garden that stopped passers-by. She had morning glories, collard greens and all kinds of stuff. She was growing her own food because that was a practical thing to do for someone who didn't have a lot of money. She also had flowers to beautify the community, so she was part of a community even though she didn't have the money that she should've had, given the kind of work she had done. Her story is not the tale of a poor, rejected, dejected writer dying alone. That was a myth that we've accepted about her because that's been written over and over again, particularly by white writers who find some romance in that kind of story of the destitute Black writer.

To get back to your question, Adam, historical fiction is fiction and imagination. You can really use historical facts just as a diving board to really dive into the story that you want to tell. I know a writer who is doing a fictional book based on the missing years of Zora Neale Hurston. There are about ten years in Zora Neale Hurston's life where she disappeared from the public record. She always presented herself as at least ten years younger than she actually was, to cover up those missing years. This writer is doing this book where she is just exploring those ten years. What was Zora Neale Hurston doing during that time?

As a nonfiction writer, as her biographer, I explored those years, but I had to base my exploration on the facts, so I was able to find one record of her during this period where she actually joined a church that her brother was a member of. I was able to explore what was really going on based on the facts that I could find, and the facts were scarce. It was easy for a Black woman to disappear from the public record if she wasn't attached to a man in some way, as either a daughter or wife.

I was able to explore those missing years based on the facts. This fiction writer that I'm talking about can do whatever she wants with that. She can imagine scenarios where Hurston was involved in a marriage, but I couldn't prove that in my nonfiction book because I didn't find any marriage records. That's why I suspected that if she was married, it was common law. I searched marriage records in seven Southern states trying to find out what she was doing, but because I was writing nonfiction, I could only speculate so much, and could only speculate based on the facts. Whereas this writer of fiction can write whatever she wants. She can make up a husband. She can make up any scenario she wants, and that's what you can do in historical fiction that you can't do in nonfiction.

Both forms are valid. Both forms are interesting. Both forms are exciting. I think we can get at different aspects of the truth by writing both historical fiction and nonfiction that engages readers of all generations.

Herb Boyd: I think Jim Frey and Joe Ellis give this discussion a whole new dimension in their fabrications. I think *Roots* again, Adam, to your good question. It cuts to the core of your concern. Here is a book that was called the *Saga of the American Family*, so he started off with a genealogical pursuit, but there are going to be these tremendous obstacles, insurmountable obstacles for him, in terms of how are you going to go back so many paths and get back to Kunta Kinte and beyond.

A lot of this is reimagined, and when you start reimagining, then you have this bleeding or morphing of fact and fiction. Of course, there is no way in the world he can even recreate conversations that Kizzy or Chicken George might have had. In all of that you have the suspension of disbelief; you have to go along with him in terms of the characterizations.

I think journalism is really the first draft of history, and that may be the distinction between creative nonfiction and historical fiction because as Valerie suggests, one is supposedly factual. It's supposed to be the real deal. No lies, no fabrications, nothing that's invented; this is how it actually occurred. Even with that, a Rashomon effect can come into play when you have nine people witnessing a circumstance, and giving different definitions of it. Nine blind men or visually impaired men, who are feeling an elephant and giving their descriptions, based upon the part of the anatomy that they are grasping, about what an elephant is. So it's always a relative thing in terms of what. in fact, were the facts.

Creative nonfiction. The nonfiction stands for itself. It's already said nonfiction, so it's supposed to be factual. The creative things are the elements of fiction that are crafted on to the nonfiction, as Valerie suggested, to enliven it, to dramatize it, to make it more compelling, more interesting. That means that you may use descriptive language that you wouldn't otherwise use in your reportage, as a reporter, as a journalist; that you develop your characters; that there is a plot here; that there is a point of view; that the whole subjective-objective thing is tossed aside. It becomes absolutely subjective. The writer, the reporter can insert him/herself right into this narrative.

When I think of creative nonfiction, I think of the late Hunter Thompson. I think of Gay Talese. I think of Truman Capote, who wrote *In Cold Blood*. I think of Norman Mailer's *Armies of the Night*. In other words, the whole new journalism school, which of course, is almost devoid of Black writers; although some of the stuff that James Baldwin did, certainly *The Fire Next Time*, and The *Evidence of Things Not Seen*, begin to approach this kind of creative nonfiction, where he gets right into a particular circumstance and brings all the elements of fiction into play to give it intensity and dramatic purpose.

Christopher John Farley: I think my view may differ a little from a lot of people in that I actually don't think there are all these genres of writing out there. I don't believe there is such a thing as historical fiction or creative nonfiction, or a lot of the other genres you can toss around. I think there are really basically two. Did you make stuff up, or did you not make stuff up? If you made something up, that's fiction. If you didn't make anything thing up, that's reporting, that's fact, that's journalism. It's something that you can accept.

Herb Boyd: [Interposing] the two things together though?

Christopher John Farley: That's still fiction, because if you make up one fact, that changes everything. If I'm writing a book about Kennedy, the Kennedy Assassination, and I say its nonfiction, but then I make up one fact, that some other guy in the crowd had a gun, that changes everything. You can't make up a fact and still call it nonfiction.

I think when you are a journalist, as we all are up here, that's the way we often perceive things. If someone comes to you as an editor with a story and says, "The story is all there. I think it should be an easy edit. I did make up one fact, but don't worry about it. It's creative journalism." I'd say, "Take off that fact you made up. I'm not going to print that. I'm not going to put that in the *Wall Street Journal* or *Time* if you made up a fact."

The same is true when you write a book. For a while in book writing, a lot of standards had gotten really, really lax; people came up with memoirs, and they made up some stuff. Editors said, "It's okay. It's a memoir. You're allowed to make up a few things. Sure you grew up among trapeze artists. You made that up, but it really adds to the flavor of your background. Sure, you said that when you were seventeen you were a Black woman, and really you're a white guy. Sure, it adds to the flavor of the memoir."

No. Did you make stuff up, or did you not make stuff up? That's all there is.

What I've written in my books, if I'm going to make stuff up, its fiction. I wrote another book called, *Kingston by Starlight.* It's based on a true story of Anne Bonny, a woman who dressed as a man, and became a pirate in Jamaica in the 18th century. That is a true story, but because I didn't know about the details of what she did, what she wore, and where she went—and I did about ten years of research—it was a novel, because I made stuff up. I couldn't make all the connections.

That's not to discount the value of that task. For instance, a lot of us probably saw *Girl with a Pearl Earring*, or read the book, which I think is a terrific book. Around the same time that book came out, there was a biography of the life of Vermeer, the painter. The biography, I thought, was not very good, because a lot of the facts of Vermeer's life were not known. People didn't know what he did or who he saw, or really what his love life was about, or his domestic life was about. The book, *Girl with a Pearl Earring,* because stuff was made up, was able to flesh that out, and I found that reading the book really took me to his time period in a way that the factual biography did not.

So I think that historical fiction has its uses, very important uses. I don't put it at a lower plank than nonfiction, but we have to make a clear distinction in order to have any kind of legitimacy in what we do. [Applause] If you're going to contradict me, you can't have the mike. [Laughter]

Adam McKible: I'm hoping we can elaborate on this. I want to go from your last comment. The word that's bubbling around in my head during this conversation is truth, getting at the truth of the past. Chris, you just made this distinction between journalism and fiction. There is something in the middle but it's—

Christopher John Farley: There's nothing in the middle.

Adam McKible: There's nothing in the middle.

Christopher John Farley: No middle ground.

Adam McKible: You said something interesting, but then maybe we can all comment on this—that when you read the more creative account of Vermeer—you felt like you had gotten closer to the truth of his world than through the dryer, less well told biography. I'm wondering if we get at—and I think about this, again with somebody like Toni Morrison, or the way that you're working on Zora Neale Hurston—if creative nonfiction or fictionalization gets at the "truth" of the past better than journalism gets at the truth of the past, what good are facts at all?

Christopher John Farley: I don't know if I said truth. Maybe I did. Maybe the record will show that. Or maybe that's your creative fictional take of what I just said. [Laughter] I don't think there is a middle ground. I think either you make stuff up, or you don't make stuff up. Again, it's not to say one is less useful than the other. A lot of people know that *Beloved* is actually based, or was inspired by a true incident that happened with a slave woman who was an escapee and killed her children. The story of Toni Morrison writing the book is that she actually just saw a clipping of this, didn't do any research, and then wrote the book. Obviously, it's a terrific book. It won the Nobel Prize, deservedly so. There are also some nonfiction accounts of that same incident that haven't been as celebrated, and deservedly so, because Toni Morrison's book was just a deeper, richer account.

I don't know if it has anything to do with truth. Perhaps this is a cop out, but most creative writers do bring events alive, whether they happened or not. They excite us in certain ways. They get us interested in looking at something more. They get us thinking about an event, but I think it's important for us to know if it's fiction or not.

When I talked about the two accounts of Vermeer's life, *Girl with a Pearl Earring* is clearly labeled fiction. It's not being passed off as, "Oh, this actually happened." No. It's fiction. It's fiction. It's a novel. It never really happened.

The Vermeer biography I read really was a biography. It wasn't trying to be anything that it wasn't. It wasn't trying to make things up. Unfortunately, it failed. Sometimes great journalists can use the facts and bring them alive without veering from those facts. It's a very difficult task to bring up, but sometimes it can happen with some of the greatest writers.

Valerie Boyd: I want to just add another example to that: Madame CJ Walker. There was a biography of her that was published a few years ago by her great-great granddaughter, A'Lelia Bundles, called *On Her Own Ground.* That was a biography based on years of research, based in the facts. About a year before that book was published, Tananarive Due, a fiction writer wrote a fictional account of Madame CJ Walker's life, called *Black Rose*. Both of those were good books. Both of those told the story of Madame CJ Walker. Tananarive's book was fiction, so she made stuff up, and she was free to do that because she labeled it fiction. A'Lelia Bundles didn't make stuff up. It took her longer to write it, because she spent 20 years researching it because she didn't make stuff up, and she labeled it, biography. Both were good books. Both had gotten at certain truths about Madame CJ Walker, and both were compelling stories. I read both books and enjoyed them both, and learned different things, and got different perspectives on Madame CJ Walker by reading both books.

It's all about story. Its how do you tell the story? I agree with Chris, either you make stuff up or you don't, and you need to be very clear with your reader, because a fiction writer has a different contract with the reader than the nonfiction writer has. As a nonfiction writer, if I'm saying its nonfiction, then I have a responsibility to you to not make stuff up. That is my contract with you as a nonfiction writer, but I can still tell an engaging story. I can still tell a compelling story. That's my challenge as a writer, to use the facts, to not veer from the facts, but to still make the story interesting. It can be done.

Christopher John Farley: I should say that I actually think that it shouldn't be seen as somehow limiting to you as a writer when you say please label yourself correctly because some of the greatest writers in history wrote historical fiction, creative nonfiction, whatever you want to call it. They made stuff up, but they had some "truths acts" in there.

One that you mentioned, and rightfully so, was Alexander Dumas, one of the greatest historical fiction writers of history who was a Black man, who took some facts from history and created incredible adventure tales that they are still making into movies. That's because of the power of his words, the power of his intellect, his ability to take facts that were interesting, and connect them with other elements that weren't true to make stories that still excite us today. That is really something that should be an inspiration to anyone who wants to go that route. That kind of writing can really live out in history.

Valerie Boyd: Also, I want to suggest a couple of other books. Herb was talking about some creative nonfiction book length works, like Truman Capote's, *In Cold Blood*. I want to suggest some by some Black writers that are more contemporary. They are book length creative nonfiction. When I say creative nonfiction, creative for me doesn't mean making stuff up. It still means nonfiction. It just means that you are writing it in an engaging way, where story, telling a good story is paramount.

Eddie L. Harris has written some interesting books including *Still Life in Harlem*, and *South of Haunted Dreams*, where he took a journey through the South on a motorcycle. He writes about that experience. He is a writer I would recommend. Read his *Mississippi Solos* and another of his books, *Native Stranger*, where he went to Africa and found himself feeling like a stranger.

I would also recommend the writing of Will Haygood, a journalist for the Washington Post, who has written a couple of biographies. The most recent one is called, *In Black and White: The Life of Sammy Davis Jr.* This book is a really personal, subjective take on Sammy Davis Jr's life, but it's based in years of research. Will doesn't make stuff up, but he tells an engaging story that just pulls you along. So those are a couple of writers that I would suggest, and you probably know of others also.

Female Speaker: I'm actually writing a book now, and part of what I'm wrestling with is—because I'm writing about my family—trying to remain true to the facts. What do you do with the family folklore that is, in fact, a fact to certain people, and there is not necessarily supporting documentation? I've been doing a lot of research. There is, in fact, conflicting history, because when you go back 150 years into the history of people of color in this nation, for those who were creating the documentation, it was not necessarily in their best interest to report the "facts." So the facts are muddied, and how do you hold to the facts? Is that nonfiction or is that fiction?

Christopher John Farley: I think you tell those stories and you mention where they came from. You mention where they are at variance with the documents that you find, because that doesn't necessarily discount those stories. What do those stories tell about the people who were telling them, or what the origins of those stories were? How were they shaped as they were passed from aunts, uncles, cousins and down through the line? That's fascinating stuff that tells us who we are sometimes even more than the documents you find that more directly nail down those facts. So I think that's part of whatever story you're telling.

It may be that when you finish the book, you think, well, maybe the best way to tell the story of my family isn't through nonfiction. Maybe it is through this fictional tale that I've created. I have to believe that a lot of the stuff that we read in Edwidge Danticat's books may be stuff that she's drawn from her family history from Haiti and fictionalized. I don't know that for a fact, but it feels that way to me, and she may have made the decision that I'm going to tell this in novel form and not as straight history. You make that decision before you publish and not when you're on Oprah explaining yourself. [Laughter] [Applause]

Valerie Boyd: I agree. I think you can write it as nonfiction, but you have to be upfront with your readers about the way the story was always told. This is folklore in my family. This story differs from this story. This aunt remembers it this way. This uncle remembers it that way. As long as you're upfront about the different versions of the story and you present it as family folklore, I think that fine to present it in nonfiction, if you choose to do it as nonfiction, or as Chris said, you might in the end decide that you'd rather tell it as fiction.

I don't think in writing nonfiction you have to absolutely know this happened, this happened, this happened in all cases, because in some cases, you don't. I don't know what Zora Neale Hurston was doing during those ten years. That doesn't mean I can't write about those ten years, I just have to tell you that we don't fully know, that the documents don't fully show us what she was doing. As long as you're upfront with your reader, that's fine.

Herb Boyd: So often in the past, people used to say tell me a story.

58

Invariably, we knew they'd mean tell me a lie. They knew that this was going to be made up, but I think one of the concerns we have is that when you're saying creative, you're just talking about the tools and the elements that go into telling that story. To what extent are you using descriptive language? To what extent is it your point of view; where is it at this point? How is the characterization? What is the plot all about? What is the dramatic intensity?

These are the elements, the fictional elements that you can draft on, or graft on to a nonfiction story or article to give it flavor, to give it life, vitality, interest and drama where otherwise it wouldn't exist.

Male Speaker: (To the panel.) I would thoroughly agree. Dead is dead. Alive is alive. That's a binary decision. Truth is truth. Non-truth is non-truth. I think that dead is dead, you cop to that from the jump, but there are different kinds of being alive. For us, those different kinds of alive become even more important. I felt very good—the previous question made me feel a little less isolated, because she is approaching an issue that I have from a different perspective.

They say that as long as lions do not have history, history will always honor the hunters. The further back we go, the less we can depend on the factual narrative, because of the inherent conflicting narratives in American History. Unfortunately, to tell our own story is contrary to the apparent fact. For that reason the "faction" as Herb says, becomes the more important, so that we can indeed tell the story, use the facts that are available, and build on those to tell the truth.

I want to get back also, Valerie, to something that you said about popularizing the history. We as writers have got to create a narrative in fact, or in fact and fiction, that is as compelling as Zane, so that the high school students who were here yesterday become as interested in Zora, or Samuel Francis or someone else as they are in the stories that Zane is telling.

There is another dimension to that, and here I want to give

Herb some props that he doesn't get in his bio in the program. A lot of the people that we want to reach, the young people that we want to reach, are using the Internet. They are using the World Wide Web, and Herb has done a brilliant job [with the web], and I hope you'll talk little bit about your presence on the web, and the role that that provides in allowing us to reach that broader, young popular audience.

So I thank you, because you've really focused on—all of you have focused on—some stuff that I'm wrestling with as I try and figure out the oral. You ask anybody, say a kid, and they won't tell you that Samuel Francis was Black. You ask any white historian in the United States, they are going to cop to the fact that he's West Indian, but that's as far as they're willing to go. Why did he later in his presence here, self identify himself in census records as white?

Those kinds of issues, I think we're inherently drawn in to. Yes, let's accept, dead is dead, alive is alive, but I think we really have to discuss the variances, and how to treat those variances. What do I do when I reach the point where my research says that this is going to have to be a "factional" story of Samuel Francis and his times? How do I treat that distinction so that people know what's real, but can use what isn't without so intruding on the narrative that it is no longer a narrative? That's one of the things I'm struggling with and I hope you all would comment on it.

Herb Boyd: Let me pick up at least a portion of Ra's statement. When you talk about the Internet, you enter a realm where fact and fiction are absolutely confused.

Male Speaker: Except on your site.

Herb Boyd: Even there, a certain amount of vetting must be done. I tell my students all the time that they have to do research papers to complete their coursework, and I drive them away from utilizing the Internet exclusively, because I get all of these websites in the citations. To a large extent you have to be very careful about the information you gather off the Internet. We've had so many problems over the last several years with misinformation and distortion that have been spread like a virus through the Internet, so you have to carefully vet all of these things. I tell them, "You can use the Internet, but maybe check that against some other sources." Check that against the published work, because really I'm a book person, so you go check out and see to what extent an individual has really thoroughly researched that piece of fact or fiction, so you can say I can confirm and verify exactly what I'm talking about. Otherwise to rely on it is to be on a fool's errand in many cases with the Internet. Be very careful about the utilization of that.

Certainly with a website we have, *The Black World Today,* I encourage all of the aspiring, emerging writers in the audience to write. You can hit me with an email and let me know what you're writing about, because it is a forum for writers who are looking for opportunities to express themselves. I shy away from a whole lot of commentaries and opinions these days. Send me some news stories.

Christopher John Farley: I want to touch upon a few things that the last questioner came up with. I edited a special issue on the life of Thomas Jefferson a few years ago. One thing that I found really interesting is that up to a few years ago, almost every major white historian did not believe that Thomas Jefferson slept with Sally Hemings. They wrote it in books. They said it in speeches. They said it went on talk shows. "He couldn't have slept with her."

Then it took a Black female historian to all but prove that he did because when Jefferson was at the plantation, he just happened to be there nine months before the birth of each one of Sally Hemings' babies. It took a Black female novelist to really take us inside the mind of Sally Hemings and show this is how it would have been. This is what she would've thought, felt and how it would've felt to be part of the situation. Then, of course, it took DNA evidence to finally just nail the case shut.

61

That is what happens with history that is right in front of our faces. You can only imagine the things that we haven't looked into with more intensity and put more scrutiny to it. In the Black community, we all knew he slept with her. When I did this special issue, I found references to Sally Hemings, how people were always remarking on her beauty, and then I saw the actual plantation records showing that he was there nine months before the birth of each one of the babies. I thought, "Of course this happened." I found that people who knew Thomas Jefferson believed that at the time this was happening, believed that he had slept with Sally Hemings, but yet in the face of all the evidence, non-Black historians were still saying, "This wasn't happening."

Again, that really should be a call to arms to people of color to say we have got to write our own histories. We have to do our own research. We have to write our own historical novels, to tell our own stories, or different stories will be told that will really not jive with what we know.

CHAPTER FIVE

The Paradox of Race and Identity

Moderator: Linda S. Jackson
Panelists: Mohammed Naseehu Ali,
Elizabeth Nunez, Emily Raboteau,
and Ishmael Reed

This panel is perhaps the most provocative of the entire Conference. Here we hear echoes of all of the great currents that have run through Black existence in the Americas. Who are we? Are we Africans, despite the fact that some of us have as much of the "other" running through our veins as anything we have brought from "Mother Africa?" Is what we have to say in our literary works meant only for Black readers as the "separate but equal" sections in Barnes & Noble and Borders bookstores imply? Or are we, as Mohammed N. Ali suggests, not a side story, stuck in a small space on the third floor, but the main story worldwide?

Linda S. Jackson: The focus of this panel is the paradox of race and identity in the literature of Black writers. The writers on this panel will explore issues such as the impact multiculturalism, diversity and plurality have on the literature produced by Black writers. They will explore the ways in which Black writers reflect and portray the complexity of their identity, and the language and concepts that may be used to conceptualize, frame and/or contextualize race in American society and the work of Black writers. These are very broad ideas, indeed, and one panel cannot pretend to provide definitive answers, but this is a conversation we must have.

About a dozen years ago, Toni Morrison wrote a very small book titled *Playing in the Dark: Whiteness and the Literary Imagination*. In it, she examines the significance and presence of African-Americans—indeed, of blackness—in the American literary imagination, suggesting that living in a historically racialized society such as America has had a deep and profound effect on American literature. She also suggests that race has become a metaphor, a way of referring to or representing forces, events and varied forms of human interaction and human vitality over time. If what she hypothesizes holds up, it certainly raises questions about how, whether, and in what ways the paradox of race, the shifting social, personal and cultural archeology of racial identity plays itself out in the literature of Black writers.

How do factors such as history, aesthetics, memory, geography, class dynamics, migration, colonialism, language, consumerism, post-colonialism, immigration and the law influence the dynamics of identity in the literature of Black writers in a society stratified by and, some might say, preoccupied by race?

We can begin to address these questions today with this panel of esteemed writers, who will examine this paradox of race and the construction of identity in the literature of Black writers.

Historians offer you facts about yourself, but I believe it is the writer who will show you who you are.

64

Our first panelist, Mohammed N. Ali is a native of Ghana, a writer and a musician.

Mohammed N. Ali: Thank you. [Applause]   Good afternoon. About 20 years ago, Chinua Achebe wrote in a book called *Hopes and Impediments: Selected Essays*, that "Most African writers write out of an African experience and of commitment to an African destiny. For them, that destiny does not include a future European identity for which the present is but an apprenticeship. And let no one be fooled by the fact that we may write in English, for we intend to do unheard of things with it."

So in these few passages, Chinua Achebe was addressing age-old issues of universality, or the lack of it, in African literature, the issue of whether African writers are capable of, or if they could document the stories of their lives in such a way for them to speak to the larger human family, as opposed to just a racial, ethnic or even religious group.

So the debate back then was, what did Chinua Achebe write in contrast to the work of, say, Wole Soyinka, who was then heralded as a universalist by the West. I believe the reason why he was given the Nobel Prize was because the West saw him as someone whose writing reflected the whole experience of humanity instead of just Nigeria. The question was whether Chinua Achebe was as capable of speaking to people in America, Russia and England as he was in dealing specifically with African issues of multiculturalism and diversity in identity.

In the same book, Chinua Achebe wrote a different essay in which he defended why he makes Africans the main target of his message and why he wasn't a big fan of the whole universalism craze at the moment.

My point in using this passage is to highlight how I believe the debate has shifted 18 or 20 years later. I see the debate as not about whether a Black writer should attempt to be a universalist, or originalist or what have you. I actually think there should not be a debate at all about what specific themes we should address as writers, because practices that we once considered as ours alone are no longer so. The truth is our culture is quickly becoming the culture of the world.

The world has shrunk in the last two decades. I'm sure you agree with me. I mean, the world is growing smaller and smaller in terms of how cultures merge and crossbreed with one another. So I believe it is even hard to define what, personally, what I truly am.

When I was growing up, I was probably watching the same television shows and listening to the same music that kids my age were listening to here in America. So, in that case, I see myself as a product of Islam, Africa, Arabia, America and Europe, which is to say, we're a lot more complex than we actually think we are, or than we actually make ourselves to be.

And I think a very important reason why Black writers should deal with issues that go beyond the boundaries of our society is because Blacks are the movers and shakers of what I call the world culture today. The biggest supporters of American culture, to me, are Michael Jordan, Michael Jackson, and Jay-Z. That is what the rest of the world sees. And this came from Black culture. It is Black culture that is going out into the world and becoming what I'm really calling world culture.

Recently, I was back home in Ghana and was reminded of how when I was growing up I watched the TV shows from America. But there was always this lag, maybe a month or two months or sometimes maybe six months later after it was in America, you would find it in Ghana, Now, anything that happens here today is seen in Ghana at the same time. And so it's really becoming complex and interesting and I actually think it's very, very positive that we have this going on. That is, we should take full advantage of this as writers so that when we document, we don't see ourselves as different or detached away from this culture.

The realities of people, of the people in Calcutta, Shanghai, Paris, Lagos, Johannesburg are quickly becoming one and of the same reality, and we as Black writers should strive for our work to have an impact, not only in our lives, but also in the lives of those people around the world because the music, art, language, poetry and, last but not least, the fashion created by us, are what is actually bridging the gap of world culture today.

So I'm going to rest my case here, and go to Elizabeth. Thank you.

Linda S. Jackson: Thank you, Mohammed. And I think the sense that I get from what you've said is that writers must take full advantage of the cultural and geographical terrain of today and not limit themselves to strictly race issues.

Mohammed N. Ali: Yes.

Linda S. Jackson: Next we have Elizabeth Nunez. Elizabeth Nunez has just published her sixth novel, *Prospero's Daughter*, which re-conceives Shakespeare's *The Tempest* on a Caribbean island, with the growing tensions between the native population and the British colonialists.

Elizabeth Nunez: Thank you, Linda. It's an honor to be on this panel with these distinguished writers.

When I look at the title of this panel, "The Paradox of Race and Identity in the Literature of Black Writers," the word that sticks out for me is paradox. And I look at paradox in terms of contradictions: What are the contradictions, what is the puzzle here about race and identity in the literature of Black writers? So I will speak to you as a Black writer and I will sort of give you a sense of how I work my way through that paradox, or how I have dealt with that paradox.

In the first place, I guess you can hear from my accent that I'm not speaking with an American accent, although I have lived here more of my life here than I have lived in Trinidad. But some things just don't get out of your skin, I guess. [Laughter] I grew up in colonial Trinidad. The only thing I knew when I was growing up in Trinidad, or through high school, were the English

67

colonialists, colonial masters who owned my island. I certainly watched my father, who I think was the most brilliant man God ever put on the Earth–which is kind of true–but I watched him hit against a ceiling over and over and over again because even though this was his country, this was his island and the island of his parents, and his parents' parents, it was owned by the British.

And you have to remember that the British who came to Trinidad weren't the brightest, sharpest knives in the drawer. [Laughter] They were definitely not, and they knew, in a quick encounter with my dad, that he didn't suffer fools gladly, so they knew in a second that they weren't the sharpest knife in the drawer.

However, I went to a school taught by Europeans. All my teachers were Europeans because the school I won a scholarship for, the high school, was made for the children of the English colonials and for the children of the plantation owners. Since I had won a scholarship, I was there. I was taught by these people. And I grew absolutely to love British literature. I found myself and I saw myself in British literature. I say to people that I used to be called Betty but when I was 13 or 14 and I had read Jane Austen's *Pride and Prejudice*, I wanted to be Elizabeth Bennett. [Laughter] I saw no contradiction, no paradox between myself and this English girl. I was she. I liked her independent spirit and so from then on, you had to call me Elizabeth.

But when I began to write my first novel, *When Rocks Dance*, I found I was stumped. I could not write this novel because any writer would tell you as my mentor   the great John Oliver Killens used to say that you can't be a writer unless you are willing to take off your clothes in the middle of Times Square at high noon, which means everybody sees you. And you've got to be ready to expose yourself to that level.

So you start to write a novel and it's a long, long, long, long journey. I'm not talking about one of these fast things you can do in six weeks. It's a long journey. It's a long journey of watching the language, of getting the ideas. And I couldn't write this novel because I didn't know what my identity was. I didn't know who I was. I didn't know what race I was. As far as I was concerned, I was English. Of course, the mirror was telling me something different.

You have to remember, my education was English, I aspired to be English and I tried to dress like the English. I tried to be everything—when I achieved that, or if I spoke like them or acted like them, I had reached the pinnacle. So how do I write a novel like that?

I faced that paradox from day one when I wrote this novel, *When Rocks Dance*; and writers would tell you that you don't so much as write a novel as a novel writes you. You may start safely writing a novel and bam-bam, the novel says, well, well, well, well, and you have to go where your characters are going if you're going to end up writing any kind of decent novel.

And where were my characters going? They were dealing with this polarization between Obeah and Christianity, specifically, Roman Catholicism. And I remembered my grandmother wasn't Catholic, she was High Anglican. If any of you know anything about the British, you can't get higher than Anglican, so she had a real attitude towards Roman Catholicism.

And I remember my grandmother used to love to tell me: you think you're so Catholic with all your communion and stuff, but I tell you what, they go to five o'clock Mass on Sunday morning, take the host, put it under their tongues and take it out in the night and make their Obeah things. [Laughter] I will never forget how destroyed I was.

When I was writing my novel, *When Rocks Dance,* there was a question as to whether there was a connection between my story and what I was told in my Catholic schools by my European nuns. There was a connection between eating the Body of Christ, between something that was transformed into the Body and Blood, and eating it. There was a connection between that and what I was doing.

So I wrote a novel to try to find myself, to have respect for African religions, and to have respect for mysticism and spirituality. It wasn't necessary for me to believe this; what was necessary was for me to respect this.

I moved from there to my sixth novel, which of course, I want you all to buy right away; [laughter] but I'll tell you something interesting about that novel. I'm back with the British here. I take Shakespeare's *The Tempest*, and I'm not necessarily doing the kinds of things that were done with Shakespeare's *The Tempest*, the novelization of it. I am trying to figure out why the heck did Prospero accuse Caliban of attempting to rape his daughter, which he uses to justify the reason why he has imprisoned Caliban. When that play opens, he justifies the imprisonment of Caliban because Caliban attempted to rape his daughter, but at the same time, he's engineering a tempest. Why? To bring a husband for his daughter. Don't you guys find that kind of funny that these two things happen at the same time? He's accusing Caliban of attempting to rape his daughter at the same time he's getting a husband for his daughter.

Something has caused this to happen. Something has made that moment happen. He's desperate to accuse this guy of rape and find a husband for his daughter. I think something has happened and that is when my imagination took off. I let my contemporary Caliban speak. I let my contemporary Miranda speak, and I think I came up with something interesting.

I just have one piece to add here. I had gotten two reviews that I think most writers would like to get: one of them in the *New York Times*, and one of them in *The Washington Post*. They were day and night. In *The New York Times*, there was not a but, there was not a however. I was on cloud nine for days, really nice. [Laughter] *The Washington Post* was dancing all around in that review. It's just like a dance, but essentially what their objection ultimately was, "Why did she have to tell us all this. Why couldn't she show us and let the book speak for itself."

This is my sixth novel, I know writers show. They don't tell. I know the cardinal rule is if you are going to be a writer, you let the scene speak for itself. You don't dictate, so I know that's not what I'm doing, but the few times I told was just too hard.

Linda S. Jackson: Thank you Elizabeth. The next panelist is Ishmael Reed, a novelist, poet, playwright and author of 20 books who has also been quite a friend and supporter of this conference since its inception.

Ishmael Reed: Thanks for inviting me again to this great conference. I was talking to Elizabeth in the Green Room there and I was noticing this morning, because I'm a C-SPAN junkie, and news junkie, that the first stories I heard were about Cynthia McKinney and this Capitol policeman. In the second story I heard about Barry Bonds messing up; Barry Bonds on steroids. I didn't hear anything about this conference. What are they trying to hide from us?

I hope you'll read *Prospero's Daughter*. Elizabeth Nunez is one of the best writers in the world. She's also very gracious and humble. I used her book, *Beyond the Limbo Silence,* in my class at San Jose State University. These are really working class white kids and Mexican-American kids mainly. They really responded to that book. Elizabeth Nunez was gracious enough to answer every student's question about that book. How many authors do you run into—they're all living in villas at the South of France—how many famous authors do you know who are that accessible?

I want to talk about the difference between points of view and fiction, and points of view in nonfiction. I wish I were writing fiction right now, because I could stay home. I'm writing a nonfiction book. I have to get those "red eyes" and travel all over the country, because I'm writing a book about Muhammad Ali, which is going to be the greatest book ever written about Muhammad Ali. There are 100 books written about Muhammad Ali. [Laughter] I think you have to do a lot of ditch digging and a lot of dull housekeeping work to do nonfiction. Your point of view is right there. If you read this book, it's going to be called *Bigger Than Boxing* and will be published in 2008 by Random House.

You'll know where my point of view is. Some traditional Black, Native American, and Asian literature, unlike modern western literature, sometimes does not hide the point of view either. It's didactic. It's used to pass on wisdom to a younger generation.

As a matter of fact, I studied Yoruba, a West African language for ten years. I have some translation in here by a work called *Igbo Olodumare (" The Forest of God")* by a writer who is considered by some to be Nigeria's greatest writer, Fagunwa. I was assisted largely by Ade Aromolaran, a Nigerian native.

Because African people teach their children through proverbs, the book is filled with proverbs: talking animals. So there is wisdom here that can probably be traced to the rain forests. You are supposed to avoid that in Western literature, which is recent in the West. Shakespeare and the Bible are full of admonitions.

In nonfiction you can tell where the author stands and sometimes in non-western traditions there exists moralizing. I think in fiction, for all you fiction writers, you have to be like a chameleon. You have to take all kind of different voices, and I think the paradox in writing fiction, and when I'm talking about fiction—I would include poetry, theatre, plays and novels—is that you might have to take the position of someone with whose position you have disagreements. Do you understand? You have to, in order to create conflict in order to have dialectic, you have to get in the shoes of a person, in the mind of a person, or character whose views might be the opposite of yours.

For example, when I wrote *Reckless Eyeballing* and it got me a lot of trouble; I had both Philo-Semitic speeches and Anti-Semitic speeches to cause tension; I had speeches that were both pro-feminist and anti-feminist. Of course, the *New York Times* only singled out the anti-Semitic speeches and anti-feminist speeches and forgot the other speeches. People who didn't read the book judged the book by those reviews. A good Jewish friend of mine, who had terminal cancer, called and said, "I read in the *New York Times* that you're an anti-Semite." When you get that label that's the end of your career. You're road kill after that. [Laughter.]

In fiction, you might have to take the voice of a historical personality, whom you might despise. You might have to take the point of view of a member of the opposite sex. I used James Baldwin's *If Beale Street Could Talk* at Dartmouth, and it was a nightmare, because women were on me everyday about all of the things that he had gotten wrong about women. His main character was an 18-year-old woman. He had her pregnant for 11 months or something, I don't know. [Laughter] It was really all messed up, and women were saying, "This is not the way you portray women. He has it all wrong." So it's very difficult to do. This is a challenge of a fiction writer. In that respect, nonfiction writers have it easy. You don't have to put yourself, for example, in a position of someone of the opposite sex.

Also, in *Reckless Eyeballing*, I got criticized because the feminist character had it both ways. She has a family, but she's also independent, and they got on me about that. I said, "Well, wasn't this the goal of second wave feminism? Having both the family a career." They jumped on me about that point of view. I derived a lot of the speeches in *Reckless Eyeballing* from feminist literature, from their novels, but I guess it's not okay when a man does it.

Black people say that you're not supposed to have plantation dialect in your writing if you're a white person. You're not supposed to do black characters. A lot of them do it very well. Others fail miserably. A very bright Black editor sent me a book by a white writer who was doing one of these white Negro or rather white black books. All of the black characters in these books are like Willie Spearmint in Bernard Malamud's book *The Tenant*.

The black characters created by white television and Hollywood scriptwriters and novelists are worse than those of Rev. Thomas Dixon and others; in fact, some of their films include quotes from "Birth of a Nation."

I don't know if you saw, *The Corner* on TV, or *The Wire*. One of the white writers, Richard Price, who says he doesn't identify with his Jewish background (nor does Eminem), and I were on a panel together, and I said, "Why are you writing this stuff? It's the same kind of stuff the Nazis use to do about Jews in Nazi Germany." He didn't get it. He just didn't have the slightest idea what I was talking about. He had all these Black people on crack. Most of the people on crack are white. They just don't get sent to prison for it, according to statistics. [Applause] Most people buy drugs from people whom they know according to former Drug Czar Joseph Califano.

We fought Bernard Malamud's novel, *The Tenant*, in the 1960s, and now they brought that thing back and made a movie of it, about an African-American writer who is so ignorant that he has to get lessons from this other writer, this white writer.

Of course, their idea of an African-American novelist is Snoop Dog who acts the role of the Black writer, Willie Spearmint. I don't know what happened, but some of these hip-hoppers just seem to lack consciousness. You see them in these movies, all these hip-hoppers in these Hollywood movies; I think we ought to apologize to Hattie McDaniel after seeing what some of these guys are doing.

I think that many members of their generation are victims of the struggle waged by Black parents for local school control, which they lost. As a result, the younger generation was intellectually flogged by a Eurocentric point of view that dominates the so-called school curriculum. Therefore, they don't know where they came from. They don't know about the battles that have been waged before.

I want to read, maybe if I have time, just a couple of short things. Give an example of how I treat that. I have in the first example—this is my *New and Collected Works*, published a couple of days ago, in 1964-2006. If you've been working on something for 40 years, you'll probably get it right sooner or later, [laughter] even if you start off stupid. In connection with this, the album just came out with some of the songs that are in here and recorded by David Murray, Billy Bang, and a whole bunch of people. It's called *Conjure Badmouth*.

I want to read a couple of things here and I think you'll

recognize the speaker. This poem is called "Notes on Virginia."

"I woke from my slumber to find her standing over me."

Notice how I'm faithful to the diction of the period and to the author's style.

> I woke from my slumber to find her standing over me. The wench held a dagger. She was about to stab me, but I seized her wrist. There was bedlam in her green eyes. Her Nigerian nose was flaring. After we struggled with the weapon from her hand, she spat in my face. Last week, I found ground up glass in my breakfast and then the mysterious fire in my study, where I was editing the Bill of Rights. Her defiance excites me, but I warned her that if her vain attempts continued, I would put her son on a spit. He was among those wretches who served dinner tonight, and the impudent Frenchmen said, 'Why, he looks like you.' He shan't be invited to Monticello again.

Linda S. Jackson: Thank you Ishmael. [Applause] This brings us to our final panelist, whose position I sure don't envy. Emily Raboteau is an Assistant Professor of Creative Writing at City College of New York and author of *The Professor's Daughter*.

Emily Raboteau: Thank you. I'm honored to have been invited to speak on this panel. This conversation has been hinging on the word paradox, because the panel is called "The Paradox of Race and Identity in Literature by Black Writers." I want to steer the conversation towards talking about how the word paradox relates to the marketing of our books.

I'm a good person to speak about this, because my book just came out, and I'm finding it to be a rather frustrating irony and a paradox that the book that I wrote, which on many levels was suppose to be an argument against racial stereotyping and pigeonholing, has been categorized as a book of African-American literature exclusively, and is being shelved in the bookstores in the African-American Study section. So you can't find my book in the New Fiction or in the Fiction/Literature section in the bookstore. I don't want to sound like I'm complaining about this for purely mercenary reasons. It's a frustration because a lot fewer people are aware of my book. Typically the only people that shop in that section are Black folks, so that's shrinking the potential readership by a really large margin, but I'm frustrated, I'm angry for everybody who is relegated to that section of the bookstore. It's a kind of literary ghetto, and you don't see a Caucasian intra-section in the bookstore.

I'm finding even when we write from a place of multiplicity and complexity, which I think is our responsibility, our books are still treated and promoted in reductive and regressive ways by the publishing industry, which is plagued by global whiteness. It's one of the whitest industries that there is, at least in this country.

It's a kind of fantasy of theirs to maintain this purity of blackness and whiteness in terms of the way they classify and catalogue books as being black. For example, we had a really hard time selling my book. A few years before mine came out there was a book by Danzy Senna called *Caucasia*, which some of you may know. Danzy looks like she could be my sister. She's like the other white looking black girl, and I guess because we look alike and we have the same racial makeup, which is to say both of us have a black parent and a white parent, it was assumed that we wrote the same book, which we did not. [Laughter]

This is what you find in the world of publishing. They will say things like, "Well, your book looks interesting, but we already have our black book this year." The paradox is that we're treated as if we haven't got anything else to say beyond race. I thought I wrote a book about a family and I'm being told I wrote a book about race and of course, I did, and it's not a mistake that I'm sitting on this panel. I'm honored to be sitting on this panel and to be allied with the Black writers that I studied. But in reviews, they might compare me to another Black writer, but they would never think to ally my writing to some of the Japanese writers, some of the Russian writers, or some of the South American writers that were also influences on me.

This is something that Jimmy Baldwin was talking about in *The Fire Next Time* when he said, "It's time to turn the conversation about race into the spaces of our own imagination."

Since this conference is dedicated to Octavia Butler, I just want to bring her up. I think she was so successful at this. She didn't create art about her race and community; rather she used her race and her community to create a body of art. I think it's our challenge now to come up with race to re-conceptualize our imaginations away from the overtly political arena. I think about how we can expand that aesthetic which responds directly to white oppression, to slavery or to Jim Crow, if we're from America, or if we're from South Africa, to apartheid. I think the more radical panel is the one that is to follow this one, the one that is transpiring today on speculative fiction, because those writers are being allowed the freedom to talk about craft and the imagination rather than just about race. I'll end there, and we can open it up to questions.

Linda S. Jackson: I'm sure everyone has at least one question, because I think that all of the panelists have presented some really interesting ideas about this paradox or seeming paradox of race, and why we may need to get rid of the notion of race and write from our experience, which I think has been one of the things that has been suggested.

Female Speaker: Hi. I think the comment that Emily made speaks right to some issues that I have. My name is Jasai Madden, and I'm the editor of a brand new literary journal, *Lorraine and James*. I know that Ishmael does a literary journal, and you've all been featured in some literary journals, so I'd like to ask all of you really, what you think the place is or what place do you think the literary journal has in expanding different conversations about not only things we said about race, but just how do Black writers fit into the literary journal landscape with regards to opportunities to talk about other things that major publishing companies might not initially allow you to talk about. How can a literary journal help expand the conversations that we're trying to have?

Ishmael Reed: I use to go around the country with a print edition of *Konch*; as a matter of fact, I used to sell them here in the audience. That was way back. I have gotten too old for that, lugging those magazines around. So I've gone to the Internet and I publish off the Internet now: IshmaelReedpub.com. I get 3,000 hits a month, which is modest, but it's far more than what you can get from a literary journal, and I cut my costs drastically. Instead of going and doing a print version, if you go on the Internet, and if you have some awareness of computer technology and software, you could do a magazine for very little. I've hired a webmaster. Our site looks good, and we're spending maybe a fraction of the cost of many other online magazine.

So I'll give an example of how with an internet site, a zine or a blog, you can present a different point of view, one other than the corporate and progressive media, which are united in their view that the problems that millions of blacks face are self-inflicted.

When the riots in France occurred, the neo-cons in the *New York Times* blamed it on gangster rap. In the current issue of *Konch,* www.ishmaelreedpub.com, I invited six French intellectuals to comment on the riots in France, and they began with the French occupation of Algeria in their search for fundamental causes. How French attitudes toward immigrants were reflective of different economical cycles where immigrant labor was needed and then when it was not needed. They presented a much more complex point of view than you find in these newspapers.

I think that's the way to go. Also, if you go to www.blogger.com, you can create your own blog for nothing. I have a blog there; so when I get pissed off, excuse me, when I become irate. [Laughter] Like this morning. So instead of just destroying my breakfast I went on my blog and commented on C-SPAN where they had two people of color putting down African-Americans. Now I'm all for multi-culturalism, but now the strategy is to take people of color, people who resemble us, to put down African-Americans. So we had two people from South Asia, who were commenting on immigration and its effects on African-Americans.

They had callers venting their racist comments coming in, and talking about how blacks don't want to work and they are all on crack, and these two guys of South Asian descent, one was the moderator, laughed along with this caller who was issuing these stereotypes about blacks. With my blog, I was able to vent. You can create your own blog. Blogger.com, it's free of charge so anybody can make a point of view.

Now to Emily's point here about African-American writers writing about politics, and maybe they should transcend that. The two most famous works by white writers are very political. *Angels in America,* by Tony Kushner rages against Reaganism. I don't particularly care for the right wing, but you cannot say that's not political. They neglect to mention the political issues covered by white writers, but always bring it up when speaking of Black writers.

That's because unlike the white writers who write about politics, black political views make them uncomfortable. I think African-Americans should have as much freedom as anybody else to write about politics. I write about politics all the time. It doesn't make it less artful. Orozco and the Mexican muralists and Diego Rivera were political, but they could paint. So it depends upon the skills of the artist. I just wanted to bring that up. Thank you. [Applause]

Female Speaker: Hi. I was in Geneva and Venice last year and a writer asked me this question and I really couldn't answer. She's Jewish and she said, if you're Jewish, no matter where you live in the world, America, Africa, you're Jewish. She knew a lot of

Africans from Africa, being in Geneva and she said in America you're African American or you're Black, but if you're an Africa American from America, somewhere else in the world, what are you? I couldn't answer the question. Are you an African African-American, if you're an African from Africa today in America? It was just a hard question for me to answer, so it's interesting with this question of identity. Then I was in Venice at a conference and I read a paper. Later on a white, retired surgeon asked me, "Do you see your characters as black or white?" I couldn't answer. I'm a black female, so they are, but it was hard for me to identify as the first— so my question is as writers do we have to have definitive answers to these questions?

Emily Raboteau: No, you write what you want to write. You treat your characters as human beings.

Female Speaker: I felt like I was asked that question simply because I was —

Linda S. Jackson: Let them answer your question. I'm not sure that they know exactly what your question is. Is it a matter of why does a Black writer have to announce his or her race? Or do Black writers announce race when they write?

Elizabeth Nunez: I guess I'm going to quote John Killens again, and the advice he gave to me. One begins from the point of specificity, and if you are true to your specific experience, your specific characters, you are writing about human beings. Quite frankly, I think this entire objection to the politics that appears in black writing is that people want to distance themselves from the humanity of the Black experience. When you write about the Black experience, and people see the common humanity, then all kinds of things break down. So what you have to say is, "Well, that's the black thing, and they're writing politics."

To answer your question, you write sincerely and as well as

you can about the specific characters and specific situation. Just as I saw myself in *Pride and Prejudice*, an English person should be able to see themselves in my Black characters. [Applause]

Female Speaker: I just wanted to say that reminds me of Percival Everett. He never mentioned race and there was a big thing about whether he should say that he was a Black man. It continues.

    This is addressed to Emily and Elizabeth. Emily had mentioned marketing and how we are pigeonholed, and it made me think of Zadie Smith, whom I adore. After the 400th review *On Beauty*, I started really thinking about it's a lot of things that go into marketing, whether it's age, race and gender; but I really started thinking, would a beautiful, intelligent, Black American woman of her age, writing like that get that kind of press. I was wondering if it was because she was British that she has gotten a lot of leeway. She had gotten so many reviews from high and low, and also deservedly. It really did strike me that I don't feel a Black American woman with her same merits would get that kind of attention. I was just wondering what you think.

Elizabeth Nunez: I'm going to go out on a big limb here. I don't think that was such a terrific book, the third one, *On Beauty*. I think you were made to read that book, because it was reviewed that well. I read it very carefully and gave it all the compassion I could.

    Now to the second part of your question, I have come to the conclusion that any writer of color would succeed in America so long as they have a white godfather. [Laughter] [Applause] You know that when Zadie Smith's first novel came, the editor of Knopf met her in England and brought her to the United States. If you look at any writer of color who has made a splash in America, they have had a white, male godfather.

Linda S. Jackson: I guess that the legacy of this Black Writer's Conference is to ferment controversy. [Laughter] Next question.

Male Speaker: It's a two-part question on the area of marketing, which Emily brought up. One is whether or not divisioning is being done by the bookstores, the marketplace, or if it's being done by the publishers. Is there any way to counteract that as a writer? As a writer you want to be read, so you want to get out to as many people as possible. Are alternatives available? Definitely, Ishmael is talking about the website. Does new media, basically, offer us a way to get our work out there in a realistic, widespread, mass way?"

Linda S. Jackson: One: Is there any hope in the commercial marketplace? Two: Do we have a chance of creating an alternative that's viable?

Emily Raboteau: That's a good question and I think you've answered it yourself. I think the answer is it's very hard to buck the commercial system that exists because it's so predominately white that it's just a paradigm of thought that's a little bit sick about how to market these books.

Your idea to think about other channels, other forms, creating our own systems is a beautiful idea, independent presses, small presses. I took my book out of this section that it was relegated to in Borders and I brought it to the manager. I said, "Just out of curiosity, I'm wondering why this book was shelved in the African-American Interest section. I wrote this book." He looked at me and saw, I guess a white face, certainly not a black one, and said, "Oh my gosh, I'm so sorry." [Laughter] I said, "I'm just wondering why it ended up there?" He looked at the back of the book and began to read the blurb. There is no person responsible. It's just the system of thought. I think the answer is to go other routes.

Elizabeth Nunez: You know Emily; I'm going to have a slight difference with you here. I have no problem about being shelved in the African American section. I'll tell you why, because African American are the ones who buy my books. One of the reasons is that I want to say to the public, there are alternatives to another kind of book that seems to be what you mentioned, the more commercial book. We write a spread of books, so I like that identification. Second, I like having the ability for the audience to come and find my book.

What I would say that I agree with Emily on is that it seems to be as though the publisher and the marketplace are saying that these books have relevance to nobody else.

Emily Raboteau: Right.

Elizabeth Nunez: I want to throw this back on you and say to you that a book doesn't sell itself. A book doesn't continue just on itself. Somebody has to take that book to the public. Now the academy used to take that book to the public. In other words, you would have your class and you would say this is the book we will read. Forget it today; the academy is only reading books written in the 1940s and the 1950s, so I don't think that's happening. Oprah is bringing the books, and not too many of you know which books, but books nonetheless. *Black Issues Book Review* is bringing the books. [Applause] *Essence* magazine is bringing the books, and you have to. If you want to talk about a war, there is a cultural war going on, because how do we get the images of ourselves and our sense of identity.

The writers I grew up on, and I'm sure many of you grew up on: the James Baldwins, the Richard Wrights, the Charles Chesnutts, the Zora Neale Hurstons. It's not that people aren't writing those books. It's that those books aren't getting published, and those books aren't getting published because you are not supporting those books. [Applause] It's a simple equation. It's simple mathematics. It's not confusing.

Believe you me, the publisher, my publisher just moved my book, *Prospero's Daughter*, which was in One World and

Ballantine, every publisher has their little imprint, just moved it to the general list at Ballantine. Do you know why? Because people were buying the book. Not because I changed. The question is if there is an audience for the book, they will do it. I hear this conversation all the time and I'd like to put it on each of us. I'd like to put that on each of us. You are responsible. [Applause]

Ishmael Reed: Let me make a comment on this. A couple of years ago, after Black America spent $350 million on books, the *New York Times* commented that African-Americans were the only group buying books during the Christmas season. Now, there are African-American bookstores all over the country. For example, in Oakland where I live, a few blocks from me is Marcus Bookstore, and they've been in business for many years.

Also on the question of politics, they approve the politics that they like. I see Shelby Steele is going to be on C-SPAN for about three hours. His Johnny-one-note theory is that African-Americans complain about their victimization too much. As a matter of fact, I was in Europe when the 2000 Election was stolen, and Shelby Steele rushed to the International Herald Tribune and said it was
a case of "Black people complaining about their victimization." Before any of the evidence of caging came in. Before investigations by Congress. Before Greg Palast and his reporting of the fraudulent way the Governor of Florida and the Secretary of State down there erased Black votes on the grounds that they were felons. They were not. No wonder The Bradley Foundation awarded Steele $200,000. This is the same foundation that backed Scotch Irishman Charles Murray's *The Bell Curve*, all about how Blacks are intellectual inferiors, a charge, incidentally that was once made against the Scotch Irish.

Charles Chesnutt complained about the marketing of his books in 1905. This was an old argument. Go read *To Be an Author* by Charles Chesnutt. They called him a voluntary Negro. He was so white looking that he had gotten into the most elite clubs of Cleveland, Ohio, because he could go back and forth, but he complains about this. His editor at Doubleday was Walter Page, who is the same editor *for Birth of a Nation*. The books came out during the same year, so you see what he was up against.

Now we have a fall back position. It's called print on demand. If you want to get a book published, you have $500; you can get a book of poetry published indefinitely, permanently. Keep it permanently in print. Go to www.xlibris.com, which is a subsidiary of Random House. You can get a novel published for $1,000.

They will print as the orders come in, so there is a fall back position, and I have a great illustration of that right here at this conference. Go out and buy the books that I published out there in the lobby. I published a book by Bodiba, a Haitian writer. It wouldn't have been published by any other mainstream publisher. It's called, *Under the Burning Sky*. I published a book by my mother, why not? She has to start somewhere, called *Black Girl from Tannery Flats*. She began writing this book when she was 74. She finished when she was 84. I went to a book party. Strangest book party I ever attended in Buffalo, New York. I had my introductory remarks, and they said they don't want to hear from me, they want to hear from her.

She spent the first half of the book party talking about her book, and she spent the second half giving messages to people in the audience from their dead relatives. [Laughter]

The other book I have out there is called *Sixteen Short Stories by Nigerian Women*. These are Nigerian women authors who are unheard of on this continent. They will tell you in the newspapers that there are only three African writers. They either write in English or French. But I'll tell you what, that continent is swarming with writers. They have book clubs all the way from Zimbabwe up to North Africa. As a matter a fact, when I came back from Nigeria, I had two boxes full of books. It was very difficult to get published over there, but those people don't complain about it, they publish themselves.

Linda S. Jackson: I guess the writers are suggesting that part of the onus is on the reader to enter this conversation by buying books by Black writers.

Female Speaker: I'd like to know what advice the panelists have for aspiring writers who don't necessarily write about the black experience. I was born in New York, but grew up in Kenya and went to school in Jamaica. My parents are from Trinidad. Like Elizabeth, I went to a British school, and I have a book of short stories. I had an agent who sent it out. Basically, she came back and said, "A lot of the publishers like your writing, but some of your stories don't deal with being black." It's hard to categorize that book because some of them do talk about the Caribbean. Some of them do talk about Africa. Some of them do talk about the United States, but there are some stories where I have not really identified the person as being black.

Again, short of publishing my book myself, I do want to eventually have a book published and no matter what I write, a lot of it is inspired by my experience, which is an African experience, a Caribbean experience, an American experience, but it's not just black. There are other things that make me who I am. How would you go about getting something like that published? What advice would you have for me?

Mohammed N. Ali: I think you should send your stories to magazines. That's a very good start. I think it always helps, because once a magazine picks it up, that's how mine happened. One of my stories was published in [inaudible] magazine, which is a relatively small magazine here in New York, but very good. That just brought the exposure, so I think you should really, really try to send them out, and just keep sending. Don't alter what you're writing. Don't let somebody else dictate what your experience as a black woman is based on what they think it is to be black, because being black is such a multiplicitous experience. I hear your frustration, but please don't change what you're writing.

Female Speaker: No, I won't.

Emily Raboteau: Yes, don't do that. Come back tomorrow and meet an editor. Meet an agent. Bring some of your work, and like Mohammed Ali is saying, send your stuff to magazines. Don't give up.

Elizabeth Nunez: Also, I think that when you say, "I don't write about the black experience." Do you have black characters in your story?

Female Speaker: Yes, some of them are.

Elizabeth Nunez: You're writing about the black experience.

Female Speaker: No, but some of the stories do have black characters, but for instance, I have stories that don't.

Elizabeth Nunez: I'm having a little problem about you letting them define for you what the black experience is. [Applause] So for you to take on that position and say, "I don't write about the black experience," is taking on their definition.

Female Speaker: I guess the better way to phrase this would be the African-American experience.

Elizabeth Nunez: Wait a minute. This is one of the problems that happens as a writer. This truth thing that I'm telling you, that Killens says, "You take off your clothes at noon." There is that confrontation with yourself in the most honest way, before you can write about characters. It may take you a lot of books to confront yourself, but when you say that you don't write about the black experience, I think that's something that you really have to examine, that you feel that you have said that. What do you mean by that? What do you mean by the black experience? If you're writing about black characters, you are writing about the black experience and you have got to believe that. You have got to have a strong belief that the characters you are writing about have relevance to people all over the world because the characters you're writing about are human beings, because they love, because they hate, because they fear, because they are jealous, because they are envious. The problem is with white people not wanting to find themselves in your black characters. [Applause]

Female Speaker: I wanted to pay homage to this conference, especially Mr. Reed. Mr. Reed just published three of my selections. My name is Rosetta. After having attended this conference, I was a reluctant writer, but I was angry. He said, "What are you going to do with that?" My latest publisher is Cambridge University Scholarly Prints. That would never have come about if it hadn't been for Mr. Reed — [Applause].

My question is for two of the panelists. Emily, there is nothing new about being regulated to the black sections in bookstores. Aesop would be there. Dante would be there, and Pushkin would be there, if they properly categorized their work.

Also, Mr. Ali, I'm worried about the prostitution of African-American culture, and the neo-colonialism of American culture abroad. I live in the United States and I live in Europe. I found that what they do is they prostitute our culture. It is not properly and respectfully presented. Are most Africans aware of that?

Mohammed N. Ali: That's a very good question. They actually are not. I tell people that what Africans do mostly is copy the worst form of American culture. There are so many positives here. In every culture you have the positives and the negatives, just like in African culture, you find something positive and negative, but they always go for the negatives. They always go for the worst things.

I speak about us writing about that and making the world

culture our culture, because we have defined it. The black experience is the experience of the whole world. At the same time, I also know it's bad the way they gobble down the culture in Africa. Again, the huge responsibility for us writers is to try to spin that in a new way, and to put it in the correct light.

Linda S. Jackson: If I could just add my two cents here. The Fifth Black Writer's Conference has been codified on a series called, *Black Writers in America*. It's been running on channel 13. Dr. Nunez was the producer of that program, so if you get a chance to see it, you should. Last night's presentation had Tim Reid. I'm sure you all know him, actor, producer and director. One of the things that he talked about is controlling our image. We have to write our story and produce our story on film. That responsibility is part of ours, as well.

Elizabeth Nunez: Linda, I'm so glad you mentioned that, because this was the last conference I directed in 2000. A television series was made of it. Ishmael Reed and I are on the same program. Thirteen half hour programs, it's all over the country. It's in every state in the country on PBS, mostly in February and March. It counters that kind of popular, commercial fiction—but interestingly the PBS programs are putting them at one in the morning.

Linda S. Jackson: Yes, they ran four of them last night, back to back.

Elizabeth Nunez: Starting at what time?

Linda S. Jackson: One o'clock in the morning, [laughter] but nobody is writing in to channel 13 to say put it on at a time that we can watch it.

Linda S. Jackson: We've got time for one more question.

Male Speaker: Quickly, I think it was Professor Nunez who noted the relationship of successful Black writers to so-called godfathers. I'd like to take it a step further in terms of the gender issue. Would you comment on the relationship of Charlotte Mason to Langston Hughes and Zora Neale Hurston, because she was, indeed, a godmother?

Elizabeth Nunez: Could you just restate your question in a way?

Male Speaker: We were talking about godfathers and the successful Black writers, so I'm asking you to comment on Langston Hughes and Zora Neale Hurston's relationship to Charlotte Mason, who happened to be their so-called godmother.

Ishmael Reed: She dropped Langston Hughes when his poetry became radical, and I think that's the problem that you get. That's what happened to Charles Chesnutt; when he's writing these minstrel things, they loved it, but then he wrote *The Colonel's Dream*, in which he asserted that slavery did not end with the Civil War and that it continued with Blacks being arrested on trumped up vagrancy charges as a way to providing cheap labor to white businesses. That still happens. The criminal justice system feeds the prison industrial with Blacks and Latinos by using frivolous traffic stops. *The Colonel's Dream* meant the end of his publishing career; that was the end of his career. That picture still continues. When I look at the residencies all over the country, where writers have an opportunity to go to and make a little money running workshops, Blacks are almost nearly excluded now. You get one or two names who are acceptable tokens, but you don't get the kind or numbers of African American writers that you got in the old days.

I want to just mention a couple of things. I was with the great writer, Joseph Heller. He and I were on a panel in Pittsburgh many years ago. Before he went on he said, "I'm not Jewish, I don't identify with that, and I'm beyond my background." Then he got up and read, and he sounded like Lenny Bruce. He did all the shtick stuff, so the particulars are there, whether you know it or not. For example, Scott Fitzgerald, nobody thinks of Scott Fitzgerald as an Irish American writer, but Edmund Wilson saw him as an Irish American writer. He said that he did things that Anglo writers didn't do, so whether or not you think that all your ethnicity and race have disappeared, outsiders can probably see those particulars better than you.

I want to end with a quote that I was surprised to run across from T.S. Elliott, who is considered the greatest poet of the 20th century, whose influence was Omar Khayyam. Not a Western writer, but Omar Khayyam. Nobody on The Great Books list. He said that all ethnic writers might not be great, but all great writers are ethnic. So you cannot separate Chekhov from the Russian experience and so on. Even though you may think that you have transcended your background, somebody from the outside might see particulars.

Elizabeth Nunez: It is not accidental that all successful Black writers, the ones we were talking about, get reviewed in *The New Yorker* and *The New York Times*. It is not because it is an incredible work of art, though it could be, but unfortunately, very often it is because of that person that you need to usher you in the room. However, we can usher ourselves in the room. That's what I'm asking for. We have to usher ourselves in the room. This is what *Black Issues Book Review* is doing.

Works Cited

Achebe, Chinua. *Hopes & Impediments: Selected Essays*. Las Vegas, Sagebrush, 1990.

CHAPTER SIX

SPECULATIVE FICTION

Moderator: Robert Reid-Pharr

Panelists: Samuel Delany, Tananarive Due, Sheree Renée Thomas, and Walter Mosley

Walter Mosley calls science fiction or speculative fiction the truly revolutionary fiction, and in particular a natural genre for a place of ideas about the imagined future, present, and past for Black people. But just what is speculative fiction, and how does it differ from science fiction? And why is one of the finest science fiction writers in the world, Samuel Delany, a virtual unknown in the Black community? And is there a welcoming hand for Black writers trying to break into this genre?

Robert Reid-Pharr: There is often the assumption that speculative fiction or science fiction, as you prefer, are either new or tangential forms within the various writing traditions within the African Diaspora. Unfortunately, I think that is still the case among people who are otherwise extremely well informed.

The truth of the matter, however, and even if we just take the history of Black American writing as one key example, is that even if you're talking about the beginning of our writing traditions, it has been the case that really from the 18th century, at least the 18th century forward, that any type of black writing that has been understood to be marginal, has very often been understood to have been speculative as well. I think it's important for us today to understand, for example, that slave narratives often came packaged with letters attesting to the veracity of the text themselves, simply because the idea of writing by any black person was understood to be actually a species of fiction, a species of science fiction, if you will.

Indeed, even today it's the case that the idea of thinking, writing, literate Blacks is understood to be somewhat outrageous, and has to be defended within science by presumably the best within science and philosophy.

Even more to the point, I know that many if not most Black writers, even today, struggle in their work too. If you will, imagine the world that has not yet come, the world in which, for example, white supremacy will no longer continue to be a sort of daily part of our realities. I am convinced then, that not only are the panelists who will be talking to us today, persons who are taking part in traditions of speculative fiction, and traditions of science fiction, and traditions of fantasy, and traditions of mystery, and mysticism, but they also continue the work of the best in our communities, say W.E.B. Dubois in *Dark Princess*, or George Schuyler in *Black No More,* even Sutton Griggs in *Imperium in Imperio.* Even figures like Harriet Jacobs and Anna Julia Cooper who dared to think that ideas of liberty, democracy, security, prosperity, brother and sisterhood were not only good ideas for elites, but for the entirety of the human community.

These comments are particularly important and indeed poignant, at least for me today. It's particularly important for us to understand the ways in which speculative fiction fits into, and continues the best of what we are as Black people, and the best of what we are as creative people, and the best of what we are as intellectuals. Especially as we mourn the passing and celebrate the life of Octavia Butler, who to my mind understood as clearly as anyone that re-imaginings of our worlds and our cultures are not important simply as entertainment, not important simply as therapeutic tools or forms of escape. But indeed, the activities and these efforts on the part of the panelists here, like those of Ms. Butler, represent the purest, I would suggest, the most serious efforts within black writing to maintain our awareness of the fact that we continue to evolve as men, as women, as Black people, as human beings, and that this is the all important first step in that process. And an important first step in achieving the beloved community, if you will.

The first person you hear today is Samuel R. Delany. Mr. Delany is the first African American to distinguish himself as a critically acclaimed author of science and fantasy fiction. Next is Tananarive Due. Tananarive is the author of seven books, including the American Book Award winning, *Living Blood*. The third panelist is Sheree Renée Thomas. She is the editor of *Dark Matter: Reading the Bones* and *Dark Matter: A Century of Speculative Fiction from the African Diaspora*. Finally, we will hear from Walter Mosley, who is the author of 21 critically acclaimed books.

Samuel R. Delany: Well, because I suppose many of us are thinking about Octavia Butler, I thought I would devote my few minutes to talking about Octavia directly. I was reminded of something when listening to Robert Reid-Pharr talking about how we want to be the best that we can be. One of the things that I think is very important in being the best that you can be, is also paying very close attention to many of the things, even all of the things that are not so good, and some of the things that would be looked at askew.

One of Octavia's finest stories is a story called *Blood Child.* She always called it "My male pregnancy story." [Laughter] That's a rather skewed notion; a man giving birth, and it's the kind of notion that I think many people would look askew at. But Octavia was a writer who was not at all shy about going for the things that look a little askew, and a little unusual.

I had the honor of having Octavia as a student. In fact, today is my 64th birthday. I'm feeling a little odd because I suddenly realize that I have now outlived probably my two best known students, Octavia Butler being the most recent, and then some years ago, Gustav Hasford, who wrote the extraordinary novel, *The Short-Timers*, on which Stanley Kubrick based his film, *Full Metal Jacket,* a very good film and a very good novel. Gus didn't make it to 35, and Octavia died at 58 last month, which is in both cases too young. What is it the Greek's said a long time ago, "Those whom the gods love die young," but it is always too young.

The first time I saw Octavia in 1970, she was a face among the twenty-odd faces around the workshop circle in the first morning of the Clarion SF Writers Workshop at Clarion College, in Clarion, Pennsylvania. By the end of my week as an instructor, my picture of her was of someone shy, sharp, and wonderfully curious. Her short story, *Crossover*, in 1970 appeared in Robin Scott Wilson's Clarion Anthology. Six years later came her novel, *Pattern Master.*

A brief decade on, Butler and I were asked to appear together in a program at the Schomburg Collection, that fabled gathering of African-American literary writers a few blocks from my old home in Harlem, where I had lived on 133rd Street and Seventh Avenue. Years before, when the Schomburg Collection had been housed in the old Bruce Branch of the New York Public Library, my mother had worked there as a library clerk. Many times I visited her there, so I felt I was, in a sense, going home.

What I found on the corner of 135th and Lenox Avenue when I went to do the program with Octavia was a brand new library building. The collection, always astonishing, had grown and been added to, and was now an affair of worldwide fame. The shy, young woman who had been my student more than a decade before had become an astonishingly articulate and awesomely impressive presence. I left the library that evening aware that I had just been honored to take part in a program with a truly extraordinary woman.

In the early part of this decade, when I began to teach Comparative Literature at the University of Massachusetts, I taught Butler's Hugo Winning stories *Speech Sounds* from 1983, and her Hugo and Nebula Award Winning *Blood Child* from 1984. I taught them again, and I taught them again. The reason I taught them so frequently was because of all the science fiction stories that we read over those years, they prompted the most interesting discussions among my students by far. Once the discussions began, again and again, the students would return to them; those tales became the benchmark text with which they judged what was going on in the other stories we dealt with.

Butler's tales became the measure for all their thinking about what science fiction might do. In 1993, Butler's novel, *The Parable of the Sower*, increased the rhetorical range, density and variety of a writerly voice that always rang as resonantly as any writer's in the country.

That was an introduction for an appearance that Octavia made some ten years ago; now I am going to read a piece just about the same length, maybe a little longer that I wrote as a eulogy for her when outside her home, she slipped and fell and died last month. It repeats some of this information but from a different point of view and a different tone.

The first I heard of Octavia Butler was many years ago shortly after I had arrived to teach at the Clarion workshop. When science fiction writer, Harlan Ellison, who had taught the week before had gotten me aside to tell me there was a student he had and who he strongly urged to come to Clarion because of her extraordinary talent. He was particularly concerned about this student and did not want her to get overlooked in the crush. Next morning, in the first workshop circle session, I noted a tall young woman of 23, who it soon became clear as the week went on, was extremely shy. When she had something to say, she said it, clearly, articulately and it was always to the point, and very clarifying, but she didn't say a lot.

During our personal conference, I remember feeling great warmth toward her and support for her. I remember liking her immensely. We shared a lot. We were both Black. We were both dyslexic, and we were both science fiction writers, but I lived on the East coast, Octavia lived in the West. We didn't see each other again for 15 or so years. Eventually however, we were both invited to speak together at the Schomburg Library of African-American Literature in New York City's Harlem.

By this time, Octavia had published several novels. It was an afternoon program and I remember how astonished, and yes, delighted I was at the way, over the intervening years, she had gained such self-confidence. She was a wonderful public speaker with a presence easy to call majestic. As I told her afterwards, it was a pleasure and an honor to appear with her.

When in 1995 she won a MacArthur Fellowship, the coveted Genius Award, I think Octavia was both pleased and a bit flustered. More than once she had said in interviews with modesty, "I'm no genius," but if we accept Lessing's description of genius from his 1756 study, *Laocoon,* genius is the ability to put talent wholly into the service of an idea. Then, yes, Butler wrote stories and novels of genius. There were lots more appearances together and all of them made me proud, in Atlanta, in Philadelphia, in New York, in Atlanta again and in Miami.

The last program we did was in November of 2004 in Washington D.C. at the Smithsonian. It was also the last time I saw her in person. In the Green Room before we went on, Octavia was drinking orange juice and we laughed together about the rainy weather outside, which did not keep a standing room only crowd away from the auditorium that night. In the Q-and-A period after, Octavia had eloquently discussed the writing process of the *Parable of the Talents*.

When the questioners lined up at the microphone in the side aisle, early on, one young man explained that he had a question for Miss Butler, and after telling her how much her work had meant to him, whipped out a sheet of paper, and asked, "My question, Miss Butler, is will you read my film script?"

After a moment of silence from the stage, Octavia said firmly, "No." People laughed, though still smiling the young man looked a bit crestfallen, as though to say, "Well, at least I tried." A moment later, more gently Octavia said, "Even if I read it, there's nothing I could do for you."

Firm, kind and wonderfully astute and articulate, Octavia made the concerns of science fiction real for many, many Black Americans as well; she used the very situations of Black Americans to give resonance and richness to many science fictional ideas. Short fiction, such as *Blood Child*, *Speech Sounds*, and *Amnesty,* one of her more recent stories, and a story in which I've heard several people state quite independently, they think might be the best science fiction story ever written, will hold their place in the canon of American thought and writing for a long time, as will the novels, *Kindred, Parable of the Sower*, and *Parable of the Talents*, among novels of ideas.

Octavia Butler is a writer and a person who is loved, who is missed. I taught her works, and her stories always produced the most provocative of discussions. I miss and mourn the woman and the writer. Thank you.

Tananarive Due: Thank you all so much for coming out on such a beautiful day, and I would also really like to an extend a word of thanks to the organizers who have worked so hard to put the 8th National Black Writer's Conference together, and I am honored to be a part of it. So thank you very much.

Whenever I see Samuel R. Delany, I am reminded of the very first time I met him, when I was mostly a reporter for the *Miami Herald* and longing for liberation. I had published one novel at that time, called *The Between*. As a result of the publication of that novel, I was invited to Clark Atlanta University to take part in something I found, quite frankly, extraordinary. It was a Black Speculative Fiction Conference. It was called the *African-American Fantastic Imagination: Explorations in Science Fiction, Fantasy and Horror*. [Laughter] I was the horror part. Among the guests, were Chip Delany, Octavia Butler, that was the very first time I met her, a woman named Jewell Gomez, who I will see later this month in San Francisco, and a writer named Steven Barnes, whom I was so impressed by that I married him about a year and a half later. [Laughter]

It was an extraordinary event, not so much for just my personal life, not only because I met such wonderful and inspiring writers, but it felt so beautiful to feel like a part of a community, and that may be a feeling many of you have taken for granted, although I think many of us at this table and others of us who are writers, or others of us who have been, feel different in some way. I know Octavia struggled to feel that she had a sense of community and her writing brought that to her.

I think that happens a great deal with my own work, because, let me just by word of explanation, I was raised by civil rights activists. My mother, Patricia Stevens Due spent 49 days in jail for ordering food at a lunch counter at a Woolworth in Tallahassee, Florida in 1960. She could have gotten out by paying a fine, but she was not going to pay for segregation, so she and other students from Florida A&M University served their sentence.

It was the first jail-in in the country as a part of the student's sit-in movement. She met Dr. King. She met Eleanor Roosevelt. My father was a civil rights attorney. They met at school, and I came from what I consider to be such a legacy of activists. I kept waiting for that activist gene to kick in. [Laughter] I did my best. I was the President of the Youth Council for the NAACP when I was a kid, and I ran for student government. I was a terrible Student Government President. I could not organize people and did not keep my campaign promises, which actually doesn't make me that different than most politicians. [Laughter]

I felt uncomfortable in confrontation. If I went to one more picket line, I was going to scream. The one thing that I had always wanted to do from the time I was four years old was to write. I was very lucky that my parents were supportive of that. They were very tolerant of the fact that I was a bit shy, that maybe I wasn't going to be an organizer. My father was more of a behind-the-scenes organizer type. My mother was more of the fire brand in front of the crowd with the rousing speeches, and I really was neither; but both of them had been writers in their past lives, before the Civil Rights Movement basically determined their futures. I was able to carry out the dreams that perhaps my parents would have pursued had not more pressing matters thrown them into the midst of the 1960s.

What would I write about? This was the question. As a child of integration, I had not been reared in the rural South of my grandmother where her father had a cotton farm. I was really raised in the suburbs; I have to say, I did not even really know anything about the urban experience that movies and television so often showed me was the entirety of what the black experience was. In grade school, I was bussed to the black school with the white kids. I was called, quite predictably, Oreo. Nevertheless, I have such a deep abiding love for my people. I was raised on civil rights stories (and songs) such as "We shall overcome." I knew them better than I knew Christmas carols. I knew the songs from the Movement, the history, *Roots*, you name it. I loved my people. My people did not always love me. That was very hard.

I remember Steve and I interviewed Octavia in the year 2000. We wrote a cover story about her for *American Visions* Magazine, and we asked her about the civil rights issue that she faced, and she probably faced it far worse than I did because of the era she grew up in, one when there was not a lot of patience for science fiction writers, when there was a revolution at hand. She told me that in some ways, *Kindred,* was her response to that, and thank goodness. Thank goodness for that response, and for *Kindred*, because that was her way.

Sometimes the metaphor is lost in the translation. Octavia was writing about our world much more than many people who might try to do it in a more literal way, through the use of metaphor, aliens, power struggles and this sort of thing that she became so famous for.

It was a very difficult question, what to write about. My mother loved horror movies, and I read Stephen King, I read Toni Morrison, but I also read Stephen King, I have to say. I did have a love for the supernatural, and for whatever reason, my stories come to me through that prism. My responses were: how do you take that experience? How do you take that history? How do you take that sense of purpose and combine it with your natural love, which was writing. My response to that was a story called *The Between*, about a man much like my parents, an activist in his community who lived in the suburbs with his kids, where their racist neighbor was throwing garbage in their backyard, (which is something that happened to me growing up), who nearly died as a child, but did not. Therefore, he lived between life and death; some people call that sort of a science fiction, alternate realities.

I think that's probably the closest I come to science fiction. I'm more of a fantasy writer. I use a spoonful of science fiction in some of my work, but mostly its fantasy. After that, it was *My Soul to Keep*, my second novel about a 500-year-old African immortal who, I had to do some finagling with to have him experience American slavery. Trust me, I wanted him to be able to speak from personal experience about what it was like to be a slave, and by the way, it really was not that long ago from someone who knows. He lived it. It was not, as so many people will try to tell us "so long ago, you need to get over that."

My response has been to try to incorporate the history that I was taught to love so much, and gained so much strength from, into a body of fantasy work that delves with everything. It's the questions that are universal questions, I think, that bedevil me as an individual. Fear of death, has been something that I thought about since I was about 12 years old. That has really kept me awake some nights. I think there is a moment when I go to sleep every night when I have that shiver of recognition that everything I'm experiencing is temporary. Whether it's this time when both of my parents are still living or as we learned so recently, that time when you had a body of science fiction and fantasy writers that included Octavia A. Butler. It had not even occurred to me that we could lose her so soon, that something might happen to my son or my stepdaughter, or my husband because I watch the news and things happen every single day.

I'm living with that constant awareness that life is fragile. As Octavia said in *Parable of the Sower*, "God is change." As I try to create characters who go through experiences I would never even want to know about, I would not even wish on my worst enemy, they teach me so much about strength and courage, that I hope I can pass on to the readers, because I don't feel like such a strong person, but I do like to create characters who are strong.

That's what keeps me going. When I hear from readers that those characters have touched them or moved them, that obliterates all the years of Oreo, all the years of wondering if I would ever fit in, of wondering where was my family and would my family ever love me as much as I love them? This is my family. You are my family. Thank you so much for inviting me to take part in this conference and I wish you all a wonderful day. Thank you. [Applause]

Sheree Renée Thomas: Good afternoon. First of all, I'd just like to thank Dr. Brenda Greene and Medgar Evers College for inviting me here. I feel so honored today, but I'll try to keep the emotions in check while calling on Octavia Butler. I feel like I'm walking with my ancestors today. I just can't believe the journey I personally made, so I'm very honored to be here with you all. Thank you.

Just want to say how I came to speculative fiction as a genre. I grew up in the South. I grew up in Memphis in a family of storytellers, probably like some of you. Some of the very first stories I remember were oral. I had grandfathers who would pass on stories to us, some stories that we wish they would not tell ever again, [laughter] but you've grown up with that. I grew up in a place called North Memphis, Klondike, which Three Six Mafia made a little popular since they come from the same neighborhood, I'm sorry to say. Not everybody in Memphis is a pimp, people, all right. [Laughter]

Both my parents were strong readers, so in my house there were books. In my house there were storytellers, so I grew up reading a lot of the Black Arts Movement writers: Amiri Baraka when he was Leroi Jones, Haki Madhubuti when he was Don Lee, and Sonia Sanchez. I also read a lot of gothic writers. Edgar Allan Poe colored my world as a young reader. My mother had some of her old text books from when she was in high school, so I read some of those works, as well. I read dusty copies of science fiction that just happened to be around, so that's how I was introduced to the field. I'm going to speed it up a bit.

I turned about 14 and, "Started feeling myself," as my grandmother would say, and began to demand more of the fiction that I was reading. I had actually read Samuel Delany's work, but didn't know that he was African American, at all. I'm thinking why can't I see my community? Why don't I see people who think and speak like my grandfather in these stories? When I do encounter these characters, why are they not in the future? Why don't they survive until the end? It's sort of like the television movies that we see, the horror movie, usually you know how that story ends. Why is the future in terms of the space opera, or what have you; why is everyone speaking with a British accent? I want to hear some Memphis up in here; do you know what I'm saying?

I started thinking about that and actually moved out of science fiction and began reading Black women writers, in particular. I was looking for Gloria Naylor. I was looking for *Mama Day* and I was looking for Toni Morrison and Alice Walker's short stories. I was reading these writers and trying to find myself in their work and give voice to my own writing.

Speed up again and I'm a sophomore in college. I was going to a small Presbyterian college, about 1400 students. Twenty-two of them were African American. Eighteen of them were Black females, so you can imagine the dynamic going on there. I took one class that was a slavery and literature class by one Black professor. All of you who are part of the Medgar Evers College here, you are part of a very important community because not everyone has that experience of going to a black college. Our teachers were brought in on a revolving door policy, long enough to take a photograph of them and put them in the Facebook or catalogue, and then they're gone by the time you register for the class that's not offered anymore.

I had to get my education on African American contributions to our world piecemeal, so I'm taking this slavery and literature class, and I don't know if this professor knew how valuable and critical this experience was, because she had us reading Octavia Butler's *Kindred*. First time I had ever read her work. I didn't know that she existed. I didn't know that her body of work existed. We read her along side Sherley Anne Williams. We read *Dessa Rose*.

Keep in mind that I lived in the place where most of the streets are named after prominent slave owners. Plantations with their historical markers say that they were wealthy bankers rather than merchants of flesh. So that's the kind of thing I grew up with, and when I read *Kindred,* it just opened up something that I didn't realize that I had been missing. I had been missing the science fiction genre, as imagined by us. I had been missing the fantasy genre, as imagined by us, and I was given a mandate by Octavia Butler to give back and see what I had missed, and what is possible. What else was there that could be added, so I'm going to fast-forward again.

I was working on a project. I don't know if you know anything about editing, but when you're editing a person's novel or what have you, you are totally immersed in their world. You are really just in their world, and sometimes you need to get out with a quickness [laughter]. You really need to just get out. So there was one particular project, I was so relieved that it was heading on out into the world, off my desk, out of my hands and into the readers' hands. I needed to take a break, and for me, one of the things that I do for pleasure is read science fiction. I know that it's kind of strange in the age of street fiction, your mama's cousin, my brother's da-da-da-da. All the little sayings that we have on some of the fiction that is out now, but I read science fiction and speculative fiction for the ideas. I read it for how it can pull me out of sight of the everyday. Because in the other stuff, I know how those stories are going to end. I was living half of them. You know what I mean? So let me go somewhere else, and that's where I went with speculative fiction.

I was looking for something in particular because when I read, I read with filters. Filters, or else if you don't read with filters, you might not read very much at all. I would read through the things that disturbed me or some of the assumptions about culture, race, class and gender that didn't really sit too well with what I knew, but just so I could get to the ideas and get to the story. On this particular occasion, I didn't want to read with those kinds of filters. It didn't mean that I didn't want to read critically; it just meant that I wanted to see my community reflected in a future that I could live in, not necessarily utopia, but one that would give me something that I could work with.

So I was looking through the bookstores, and I usually go to the independents, but I read all the black sci-fi books that they had. At that time I had discovered Tananarive Due's book, *The Between*, because my mentor, publisher Cheryl Woodruff had given it to me and said, "I know you like that sci-fi stuff. Let me get you to read this."

I read it right away, and then I went online, I looked for Tananarive Due and was astonished to find that she was a part of this woman's writers' organization or a book club. She e-mailed— she probably doesn't even remember, but she e-mailed me back and I was like, "Wow."

I read Steven Barnes' books and I was like, "Where is his next one? He's not writing fast enough"; and Octavia Butler. I read all that I could find, except for *Survivor.* At the time, I didn't know that existed. Samuel Delany was writing *Autobiography* and his amazing *Literary Criticism*, which I had to struggle to get through because it's so brilliant. But I was like, "Where is the fiction?" I felt like I had reached this dead end and I was like, "Surely, I can get their short stories."

I know that Steven Barnes had written short stories. Surely I can find it in a volume. I didn't know where that book existed. I asked all the book associates, "Do you know of a book of black science fiction? Do you know a book?"

"Have you read *Bloodchild?*"

"Yes, I have read *Bloodchild.* Yes, I have several copies of *Bloodchild.* What else do you have for me?"

So one of the book associates at a Barnes and Noble sent me to a Martin Greenberg anthology that he co-edited on Japanese science fiction, and it was 10 stories that had been translated from Japanese into English. I took that home. It wasn't what I was looking for, but it was something interesting, so I took that home and I read, I think, three stories and I woke up about three in the morning. I woke up a little mad. I woke up a little upset, a little disappointed. I thought, these are good stories; these are good stories, but somebody took the time translating these Japanese stories so I could read them in English. Why isn't there a volume of black science fiction of people who are already anointed and celebrated and cherished and have won every award that you can think of? Why isn't there a volume of this work out there? What about the other writers that I don't even know about or that don't get articles in the magazines, and what have you? What about these other writers?

So the seed was planted. I will just say this that Octavia Butler and Samuel Delany were very, very generous in supporting the work that I did for *Dark Matter.* Initially, the *Dark Matter* series I imagined was just going to be reprints of stories, but someone at WBAI, I think it was Mike Sargent, told me, "You better get your little self down to the Manhattan Theatre Club, because Walter Mosley and Octavia Butler and Jonathan Lethem will be there reading and perhaps you can talk with them about your idea."

I didn't even have a title for the anthology at the time. I didn't even really know it could be an anthology. It was just something I was just kicking around inside myself, and if Marie Brown hadn't encouraged me to pursue this idea, it probably would have been just another note to myself in my journal. I remember talking with Walter Mosley and I don't even know if he remembers. He gave me this funny look, like, "Oh, Lord. She wants to do an anthology and I just got my first science fiction novel published." I remember that, because he ended up going to a different house to get it published, and this after being a national bestselling mystery author. His editor was looking at me like "Don't come to me, please." While I was talking with him, Betsy Mitchell who was publishing at Warner Books at the time, literally pulled my elbow, pulled my sleeve and said, "Bring it to us, let's talk. I see. I get it. I get what you're talking about."

And Octavia Butler was so supportive. She said, "I will see." She has this beautiful Julia Child voice. It reminds me of elders back home. She said, "I'll see what I can find for you. Perhaps I have an essay that might be good for *Dark Matter.*" And she did not forget. She did not forget.

So I just want to say thank you. Thank you to each and

every one of you up there. I appreciate it. You are the shoulders that we're standing on. I've worked with writers at the Frederick Douglass Creative Arts Center. I was blessed to have the opportunity to teach African writers in London with Kadija Sesay, editor of *Sable* magazine and I want you to know that that community, that maybe we're not so aware of, is larger than we think. There are people who are out there writing stories, people who are creating the world in the image that they would like to see, and also people who are writing tales that are lifting their communities. That's what I'm interested in. That's what I'm doing. That's why I do the hard work of working with crazy, talented writers and the work on science fiction. Thank you.

Walter Mosley: Thank you. Hello, everybody. Most fiction is conservative in its nature. People write books in order to codify things, in order to belong to things, in order to interpret themselves through structures that already exist, language, ideas, nations, peoples, genders, all kinds of stuff. It's not that all fiction, that all writing is conservative, but a lot of it is. A lot of it exists to either support something that already exists or to join that something, to be part of it. Much of our writing is that. Many of our writers do that. The Black community is also a very conservative community, a very conservative people, and very religious people, people who have been kept out of the mainstream even though we have been the mainstream, from way back in the beginning.

The only form of fiction that I know of that is truly revolutionary is science fiction and speculative fiction. I understand it like this: If you are a radical lesbian feminist separatist, and you want to write a novel, you should write a science fiction novel. You could say, in the year 2267, there were only women on the face of the Earth. [Laughter] This is a revolutionary act, right? It's a revolutionary act in writing. All right, and only Black people left. Not only is it revolutionary to mean to say it overthrows a way of thinking; it also puts pressure on you to figure out, what are you going to do now that you are here? Is everything

109

fine? Is everything perfect? Black people all get along? Women all get along? There is no more trouble?

I was invited to a meeting of the elders. I didn't like the idea that I was invited to this meeting, but Harry Belafonte called me and he said, "Walter, I'm having a meeting of the elders, and I think you should come."

I said, "But, Harry."

You don't really say no to Harry. He said, "Come," and I said, "All right, I'll go there."

It was in Atlanta and, at the same time, there was a science fiction conference in this hotel, in the same hotel where we were having a meeting of the elders. The elders were Sonia Sanchez, Andrew Young, one of Martin Luther King's teachers, Louis Farrakhan and Al Sharpton. There were like 80 people. It was wild, and these were some serious people.

Then the science fiction conference—I don't know if you people go to science fiction conferences. The men dress like Vulcans and the women wear no clothes. [Laughter] It's wild. "You see my breasts? They're for nerds." [Laughter] Thousands of these people—thousands of them, and on top of that, there is the 30 or 40 members of the Nation of Islam, being bodyguards, and then there is Andrew Young, Sonia Sanchez and Harry Belafonte getting all the Vulcans together to sing Deo. [Laughter] I'm not making this up. It's true. [Laughter] It was a wild notion. I mean, it was wild. It was kind of beautiful because you don't even discuss—you couldn't even think that you people are mixing together, they just are, and there is no difference between them because all of them are so wild.

It was a really amazing event, but at one point, Harry was saying that the last time that he had gotten together with Martin Luther King was in his apartment in New York. They used to get together, all of them, and they would make planning sessions. How are we going to deal with this? At one point, Harry had said that Martin Luther King had turned to him and said, "I'm bothered."

All of them asked, "What's bothering you?"

"Well, I feel that we are integrating ourselves into a burning house."

It was moving. He was dead in a week, but he would say, "I feel," and they would say, "What do you think about that? Have we done the wrong thing?" He would say, "No, we haven't necessarily done the wrong thing, but I think that we're going to have to become fire." One of the people there—a lot of people started talking about that at the elders meeting. One person said, "I think we should just let the house burn down." That's a science fiction notion right there. Let's let the house burn down and see what we have left. See what's there. See what we can build. Black people can't have fiction without science fiction. We have to make up shit. We have to make up shit, because everything was taken away, right? Our language, our history, our religion, our freedom, and then we came here and we did all this great stuff, George Washington Carver, this great genius. Nobody even knows who he is and they'll say, "Didn't he invent the peanut?" Do you understand? Well, anyway.

So what I'm saying is that I'm trying to be aware of the fact that it's wonderful that people are starting to pay attention to science fiction. Of course, we've been reading it forever, reading comic books, reading science fiction. All of us have, because we can get away from this world that is so oppressive to us, but on the other hand, I want to be aware that there is a great deal of conservatism. There was a lot of not-so-positive response to letting the house burn down in this conversation that we were having, even though all of us knew that probably we should.

But we're afraid of what will happen. What will happen if there are only black people on the face of the Earth? What are we going to do? How do we live without the whites? Can you imagine being a slave and being freed? How do I live without the white man? I don't have any idea of how the world works. It's true. What am I going to do? They used to feed me. Now what am I going to do? Now what?

I think there are problems that we have to face in order to

deal with our creativity, with our courage, with our revolutionary urges. And those urges don't have to deal directly with any kind of racial issues. Also, I want to say and I need to say that there is a great deal of genius that we don't pay attention to. I was thinking about that Oreo thing when I was a kid listening to Jimi Hendrix, and how most black people would say, "Oh, that's white music." I would say, "No, that's the blues." They would say, "Yes, white music." We didn't know. I knew it wasn't white music because Jimi Hendrix wasn't white, but it's not that I understood what the blues was exactly.

Octavia told me a story once. She said that she had these neighbors and they were scientists, and she had one of her books. I don't remember which one, maybe it's *Kindred*. They said, "We hear you're a writer. We'd like to see your writing." So she gave them *Kindred*. A couple of weeks later they hadn't said anything, so she said, "Well, have you read my book?" They said, "Oh, we looked at it and we saw that it was science fiction so we gave it to our children."

At that moment Octavia said, "I'm going to stop defining myself as a science fiction writer." Otherwise, she saw where she was going. There is a lot of recognition of Octavia, maybe more than any other science fiction writer in America—maybe. Still she lived like she was being excluded.

I just want to say in ending this that it's a nice thing to be able to say good things about Octavia because she was a love. She was a wonderful person. I used to love kissing her, because she hated it. [Laughter] I'd say, "Hi, Octavia." And she said, "Oh, no, I have a cold." I'd say, "Octavia, you've had that cold for years." [Laughter] But she was wonderful. You had to love her. I think she liked it that I wanted to try to kiss her.

We have Samuel Delany. I just wanted to say that this is one of the greatest men in American literature. [Applause] Taking nothing away from Octavia, Mr. Delany is it. He's the joint. He is like the center. He is one of the most amazing writers, thinkers, and revolutionaries, in that literary sense, that America could have. He belongs to us and most of us don't know it. Let me put it like this—many of us don't know it and even those of us who know it, don't know how to celebrate it.

This man is great. He is like a senior professor with tenure, and I don't think he went to more than a semester of college in his life. They couldn't say no to him, because this was Sam Delany. He was black, but they still couldn't say no to him. They said, "Damn, he knows more than all of us put together." He does, really, what he knows, the depth of his knowledge, the depth of his ability, the incredible beauty of his work. Really, one reason that I'm saying this is in order to honor Octavia. I think she would want us to pay attention to what we're doing and what's alive today with us. You're sitting here in the room with one of the greatest men in American literature, period. [Applause] And thank you.

Robert Reid-Pharr: Thank you all very much. I want to ask one question. I want to know if it's actually true that there are more black persons who are entering speculative fiction and science fiction than when you began?

Sheree R. Thomas: I will say this. *Dark Matter* came out in 2000. *Dark Matter: Reading the Bones* came out in 2004. I'm still receiving submissions for the first one because the Internet is amazing. We were talking about truth and accuracy in the earlier panel. It's still on the Internet somewhere, and people still are asking me if we're doing it. And some of the writers from the first two volumes have continued to publish their stories.

I have one writer right here, Andrea Hairston, who just published her novel. I believe it's the first novel that's coming out of the *Dark Matter* books. It's *Mindscape*. I know there are several others in the pipeline and I'm editing a third one on Africa, so we'll see what's happening, but there are about five different black science fiction lists that I know of on Yahoo Groups. And there are different organizations that are pulling together. There is a Carl Brandon Society that celebrates the speculative fiction work of writers of color, so we're trying to reach out to each other. So yes.

Robert Reid-Pharr: Okay, we can take a question here.

Female Speaker: Yes, first I want to thank everyone for their contribution. I have a two-part question. First, I'd like to hear something about the province of speculative fiction versus the idea of science fiction. Is it important to talk about calling it something other than science fiction and fantasy?

    The second part of my question is to Samuel Delany. When you started it must have seemed to almost have been a wilderness in terms of support, role models, etc., so I'd like to hear more about the genesis of your getting involved in writing. Thank you again, everyone.

Samuel Delany: Do you want to take the speculative fiction?

Sheree R. Thomas: Oh, the speculative. How I use speculative fiction for *Dark Matter* was the way I thought Samuel Delany and Marilyn Hacker used it when they edited a wonderful volume called *Quark*. That's where I found the term, and I liked how they used it there. I thought it worked well with what I was trying to do with *Dark Matter*. Speculative fiction, for me, is an umbrella term, which I believe was coined by Robert Heinlein. Science fiction explores the way technology and the natural sciences develop over time. Heinlein thought that there should be a word that explored a body of work which discussed how maybe cultural values, traditions and languages, things like that, might change over time as opposed to just the technology, so speculative fiction was used in that way. For me, it's an umbrella term that includes science fiction. So I could have stories where the science is so critical to the story, if you took the science out, you wouldn't have a story anymore. Or fantasy stories where you have works where the writer has created a world where they have their own internal logic and magic, or magical realism, however you choose to define that today, or folklore, horror, things like that. All those different types of writing fall together under speculative fiction, that is, non-mimetic work.

I knew that I wasn't going to be able to get a book full of space operas and such for *Dark Matter*. It's hard to get it for any writer. I think Gordon Van Gelder, editor of *Fantasy and Science Fiction Magazine*, told us at Clarion West (a noted science fiction writers workshop based in Seattle) that if you could come out writing "hard" science fiction, science fiction that lets you explore the natural sciences, then you can rule the field, because there are editors who are constantly looking for good, hard science fiction. But I knew I was going to get folklore, retellings, horror and different things like that, so I wanted it to be open. I didn't want to close this narrow door that was really just beginning to open up, so that's why I chose to use speculative fiction and it's worked well for me.

Samuel Delany: Sheree has just given a wonderfully accurate description of what speculative fiction means. The only thing I would add is that it's a term that I used for about two and a half years back in the end of the 1960s, the beginning of the 1970s. At around 1971, a small group of people within the science fiction community was using it the way Sheree has just described to you. It kind of moved outside of that community, and it went in two directions.

One, anything that was science fiction dropped out of the meaning. Anything that was fantasy dropped out of the meaning, and it was only used for experimental fiction or magical realist fiction, the stuff that didn't have a category already. I didn't think that was a particularly good development. Then it also entered the Academy at about that time, and basically the people in the Academy used it for any science fiction they liked. [Laughter] Any science fiction they did not like wasn't speculative fiction.

That's kind of like looking for this black community, but

we're only interested in the authentic Black people. We're not interested in anything that is impure. We have an example of that. We have many historical examples of that. That just doesn't work. So I dropped the term and I went back to the more conservative term—science fiction. As long as people use it the way Sheree uses it, I'm perfectly happy with the term, but I tend to use the more conservative term—science fiction, fantasy and experimental fiction using science fictional images. When you put it altogether that's science fiction.

The woman asked specifically what it was like in the beginning in terms of support. There wasn't any. In one sense, at least there was not a great deal of support from the black community per se. The science fiction community, however, has always been a fairly liberal community, largely Jewish, largely on the left, and largely sympathetic to things new, so that when I came in, within the science fiction community, I was the only dark spot in the mix.

Nevertheless, there was a certain amount of welcome. Not a huge amount, but there was a certain amount. My grandfather was a slave. Not my great-grandfather. Not my great-great-grandfather, but my grandfather. Emancipation came when he was 7 years old in 1865. Then you realized, let's say, Paul Robeson going into law school at Columbia. That was 86 years ago when he went in, and 86 years is a single person's lifetime. There are people who remember what went on 86 years ago, many people. We have grandparents who remember that, and when Robeson went in to Columbia Law school, whenever he would try to speak, all the students would stamp their feet loudly so that he could not give his talks, and the professor encouraged this and thought it was really great that he should be stamped out, that his words should be stamped out. He had to stand outside the classroom and corner the ringleaders and threaten to break their heads if they didn't stop. As I said, that's 86 years ago, one person's lifetime ago. It's not that long ago, and it's very important to remember that.

You said so kindly, Walter that I know a great deal. That's

the kind of thing that you have to know about: where you come from, what happened to the people around you, the people around your parents, and that gives you power. At a certain point, you just decide, I'm going to do what I want to do because I have to. That's the way I broke into science fiction. I read it. I liked it, so I thought, I can write it too. That's basically how it happened.

Robert Reid-Pharr: We'll take this gentleman to the right.

Male Speaker: Yes, thank you very much. This question is for Mr. Mosley and everybody present. In pursuing this whole idea about race, how to resolve this and move this whole issue to another level, I've embarked upon a project that I think has great significance. It is a film based upon the works of J.A. Rogers, *From Superman to Man*. I think J.A. Rogers did a very creative thing in taking this whole argument about race and putting it into this little scenario between this porter and this racist, white supremacist senator from Oklahoma. Growing up in Birmingham and seeing the whole horrors of race up close and personal, I guess I just took off on this as a project. I am trying to move it to film, Mr. Mosley. I wanted to know if you could give me some feedback on how you were able to move your story from a book, a novel, into the film arena. If you could expound on that, I would be most appreciative.

Walter Mosley: I'd be happy to, not that I know anything. The way I understand the film world and the literary world is this. About 60 or 70 percent of all books are options for films. Everybody in the world wants to make a book into a film. They are always looking for it. They are always trying to figure out why it's not going to work. They are paying you, and they're not doing it. I made a movie, *Devil in a Blue Dress*, based upon my first book. It was a very successful movie.

It didn't make a lot of money in the box office; it kind of broke even. But in videos, man, every brother in the country has that film, and they don't even know Don Cheadle's name but "That guy,

117

that guy who plays Mouse." They made all kinds of money on that, and it wasn't actually about two months ago that I signed a contract to make my second EZ Rawlins film, so it's been about 10 years. It takes a very long time because people are very frightened.

I can tell you exactly what they're frightened of—it's an interesting thing. They're frightened of not spending enough money, and they're frightened of spending too much money and losing it, so the thing is that if you publish the book, people are going to be looking at it and paying attention to it. If they have an agent, they are going to help guide you into that thing, but then the question becomes of making the film something that they can imagine spending the right amount of money on, and that they can make money back with.

It's a very difficult thing and I don't understand most of it. The thing is that I just keep trying and trying. Sometimes it works out and sometimes it doesn't work out, but the book itself, having the book is a big thing. Then after that—seeing as you're trying to make a project, I suppose you are going to have a screenplay. Having a screenplay is a very important thing. They have something in their hand that they can reject. Let's be honest. Most people are going to reject it. It's like writing. You get 100 rejections and somebody publishes it, but then you're published and 100 rejections don't matter, but they need stuff to work with. And you're making the stuff, so it's going to work. Let's be positive.

Robert Reid-Pharr: Unfortunately, I have to say that we only have time for two more questions, so we're about to run out of time, so we'll take the first person there and maybe the last three of you can do some horse trading.

Female Speaker: I actually had two quick questions. Even though most of your works have African American characters, do you find that the science fiction community is more colorless, so to speak, or that it's less of a paradox of race and identity? This is kind of a follow-up question from the last session, at least as far as your acceptance in the wider community.

Next quick question is—I was at a meeting recently where *47* was introduced as the first science fiction book by a black person intended for young adults. The question is simply, are there plans for any more science fiction books by any of you geared toward young people?

Sheree R. Thomas: Hi, I'm just going to pick up from the young adult literature. Virginia Hamilton, I believe, would be the first author to write a series of books for young adult readers, including science fiction. If I'm not mistaken, she's also the first science fiction writer period, to get the MacArthur grant because she did the *Julius and Her Brothers* series, which is a wonderful trilogy. She's probably most well known for her retelling of *The People Could Fly* and *Her Story*, so definitely look at Virginia Hamilton's body of work. *47* is wonderful. I actually taught *47* last summer as an Artist in Residence here in Brooklyn at the Weeksville Society. I have a workshop I do with teens, where we use science fiction and the history of that community to help young people explore speculative fiction and the history of Brooklyn, so we used *47* for the first time. That was wonderful. They were looking for you, Walter, but that's all right. There is an African writer, Nnedi Okorafor-Mbachu. Sorry, I had to think about how to say her name. She's in Chicago. She has a new book called *Zahrah the Windseeker* that just came out.

Walter Mosley: Thanks. Show off. [Laughter]

Sheree R. Thomas: [Laughter] But I did it. It's a wonderful volume. Nalo Hopkinson is an Afro-Caribbean Canadian writer whose books have been taught both ways. They're for adults and young adult writers: *Brown Girl in the Ring*, *Midnight Robber*, maybe not *The Salt Roads,* but definitely those first two books. She has short stories as well. There is some work out there. Are you working on something for young adults?

Tananarive Due: No. Really quickly, I wanted to address the first part of that question in terms of acceptance, and I'll be really quick because I saw the wrap up sign. I know that for both Octavia and my husband, Steve, in the science fiction community—their books were published with white faces instead of black faces on the covers, which will speak to what the publishers thought the public would buy, or not buy if they knew the truth. Now you will notice there were a lot of reprints and new editions of Octavia's work with very African looking black faces, so times, they are changing.

I have had acceptance in the horror community overall, and it's a growing acceptance of what I would call mainstream readers, maybe white readers who don't consider themselves horror readers. My core community has always been Black readers, Black female readers in particular, but Black readers.

Female Speaker: My question was going to be to you, Walter. How do your characters remain human, particularly maintain their humanity, particularly Socrates and some of the other characters that we see in your other novels?

Walter Mosley: My answer should be thank you because that's the thing about writing about characters. They should be human, and so I think that the biggest problem that writers have is loving their characters, but it's also the most important thing. You have to love your character. I mean to say you have to understand them. You have to understand how they're feeling and where they're coming from. I just wrote a story about a youngish Black nurse and an older white man who is dying. She's taking care of him in his house. It comes out in a period of time that he murdered a Black man, because he forced the Black man's wife to have sex with him, and he was afraid that the wife would tell the man, so he murdered him. This was 70 years ago. He's old and he's dying now. This Black nurse is taking care of him and he's scared for obvious reasons. The hardest thing to do was to understand this poor white cracker's view of the world, and why he felt he had to do this thing. I think I was capable of doing it. I think that there is even a tiny little moment of understanding who he was. I don't think many of my readers are going to forgive him, but that's the world you live in and you have to understand your characters.

I'm just going to say that the other thing is it's hard to feel responsible and to understand the language and the brilliance of young people. In America today, there is a lot of brilliance in the community. There is a lot of understanding and there is a lot of reaction, especially in the conservative communities like ours against their expressing themselves and learning how to express themselves, and feeling comfortable expressing themselves. Our biggest job is to allow young people into our world by saying who they are, not who we want to hear who they are. I think if we can do that—reading is kind of waning anyway. I'm not saying that we can do anything about that, but I think we can do a lot about making the room for young people to be part of our world, and in so, making it their own world.

Samuel Delany: I just wanted to address the question over on my right, because I think it's a very good and important question. The way I would respond to it is to say, right now, and it goes to what Walter was saying about our living in a very conservative world. The media is extremely exciting. It commands millions and millions of dollars. It's something that we all are interested in. Study the media. You will learn lots and lots about art.

However, because we are going through this conservative time, the media is not where you go to learn about life. Where you have to go to learn about life is still what's written on the page. So if you want to learn about what's going on in the world, you must read. That's the only way you're going to get that.

You learn, as I said, all the stuff about art you want to know— looking at movies, television, and listening to rap and what have you, but if you want to learn about what's going on in the world, you have to open that book and read it. That's all I can really say.

Robert Reid-Pharr: Thank you very much. Before we go, I wanted to remind all of you that we are in a space that is dedicated to Medgar Evers and that Mrs. Myrlie Evers-Williams is the Honorary Chair of this Conference. Mrs. Evers-Williams is indeed in the auditorium with us now, as is her daughter, Reena. [Applause]

Mrs. Evers, thank you so very much. You make us all of us extremely proud, probably more than you know. I also wanted to take this opportunity to thank our panelists, Samuel Delany, Tananarive Due, Sheree Thomas, and Walter Mosley.

CHAPTER SEVEN

The Writer as Literary and Cultural Artist

Moderator: Carlos Russell
Panelists: Steven Barnes, Carl Hancock Rux, and Camille Yarbrough

In many ways this panel neatly handles many of the themes raised in the other panels. However, it also raises another provocative subject heretofore not dealt with: that is, the sometimes seeming disconnect between the older "Civil Rights" generation who saw art as a political weapon to be used to gain group liberation, and the Hip Hop generation, who see art as a tool for individual self expression, as a way to gain personal fame and fortune, and as a career path that will enable them to have the ability to support a family.

Carlos Russell: Perhaps the best way to begin is by simply saying, Hotep.

Audience: Hotep.

Carlos Russell: Abadi Jambo. Good afternoon. Bonjour. I welcome you to this panel, "The Writer as Literary and Cultural Artist." I do so, in as many greetings from our African Diaspora that I have a modicum of acquaintance with. And I do so for a particular reason. It is a symbolic way of reminding you that irrespective of where we were born, we are one people.

Before he died, John Oliver Killens, who was my neighbor, and who I knew during my days as a member of the Harlem Writer's Guild, which at that time he co-chaired with John Henrik Clarke said to me one morning as we were having breakfast, "Carlos, if you want to know where a people are going, just look at the artists." In other words, for him, the artists are the people that define the future of the people from whence they came.

As you all know, this panel is dedicated to the memory and work of the great, late August Wilson. And I would hope that you would share with me that wherever he is, he's now with the ancestors. It is appropriate that that was done, for his life was one of struggle to project and promote the notion that the artist is indeed an integral part of the cultural matrix from which he or she comes. I am certain that some of you are well aware that he had to go through a long struggle because there were those of the European persuasion who would argue against that role. So if it is true that John Oliver Killens is correct, that a people are best known by their artists, then when one sees and reads the works of August Wilson, one could look clearly at the direction in which the people should be going.

This panel then fits squarely, in my judgment, within that context. Because what you will note is that there is a common thread among the panelists.

In addition, before I introduce them, I want to say to you

that one of the things that I believe is that we rarely think things through, that what we try to do, generally, is to respond emotively to ideas and concepts, taking them prima facie, without digging deeply into what is behind them. And very often, we expect to hear what we want to hear rather than what we need to hear. Hopefully, and after having read the bios of the panelists, I am certain that they will share with you what, from their perspective, you need to know, not necessarily what you want to hear.

The first panelist to my far right is Nana Camille Yarbrough. She's an educator, a performing artist, an actress, a dancer, a singer, a choreographer and a composer. She has guest-hosted radio programs for Bob Law, Carla Bird and Carlos Russell. She's the host of her own television program, *Ancestor House*. One of her most critically acclaimed works, *The Iron Pot Cooker*, was her first album. I will also mention a children's book, *Cornrows*, that I view as perhaps seminal in the works of books that reflect our reality for children.

Brother Carl Hancock Rux is a multi-disciplinary writer, once described by *The New York Times* as one of 30 artists under the age of 30 most likely to influence culture over the next 30 years.

Steven Barnes has published over three million words in fiction, including the Endeavor Award-winning *Lion's Blood* and *The New York Times* bestseller, *Beowulf's Children*.

Many years ago, when I was an associate editor for *The Liberator* Magazine, (*The Liberator* and *Freedomways* were the primary journals in the 1960s that expressed concepts looking for positions that would reflect the political realities, social realities, and economic realities of Black America) they held a conference in Harlem and it was called "Must the Black Writer Lead?" This evening, with this panel, I would like, with your indulgence, to do it slightly differently. I would like to phrase a question and then ask the panelists to respond individually to the question from their perspective. We will get an opportunity to interact with you, the audience. And you will be included in the discussion and in the dialogue with the panel in the African tradition where the community converses around essential issues. So that is the process that I would like to employ, if it's okay with my panelists. Is that fair? Is that clear?

Panelists: Yes.

Carlos Russell: Thank you very much. Here is the first question. You are dancers, writers, actors; the question is, to whom is the cultural artist ultimately responsible? Is he or she responsible to the larger society? Or is he or she responsible to the community that spawned him or her? And, if so, is there a contradiction?

Steven Barnes: Okay, the primary responsibility of an artist in my mind is to express their deepest essence, who and what it is that they are. That starts just with the miracle of existence and moves from there to being alive. And moves from there to perhaps questions of race or gender, depending upon where that sits in their hierarchy of values. As an artist, you understand that there is a feedback between the works that you create and the community that provides you with sustenance. I mean; I like to eat. I like to have a roof over my head. So I have to take into account the question of whether or not my work is rewarded financially.

But when I do that, I have to ask myself the question, what is my responsibility to that artist—to that audience? That is why I, as novelist, for instance, learn forms of various kinds, things that have to do with plot and characterization and so forth if I'm writing novels, questions that have to do with the novelistic form as opposed to when I work in television, which has to do with creating stories as sequences of visual images.

But the question of art is not separate from the question of who I am, as, let's say, a martial artist? That's another important part of my life. It's the question of expressing myself through physical motion in interaction with another person.

So it keeps coming back to that question of, who are you? Which, in many ways, is the only really important question, or is

126

one of the most important questions for people to answer.

One of the things that we are is represented by our interaction with our community. It just has to be that way and to the degree that you feel that, then it is appropriate for you to express that. If you don't feel that, you shouldn't bother trying to express that. I know, for myself, I cannot escape that, because I know the amount of pain that I felt being excluded from the cultural conversation. I did not see men of my own ethnicity being treated as if they were intellectual, courageous, honest, sexual beings. And it hurt me terribly. And it created wounds that took decades for me to heal. For me to not address that in my work would be moral cowardice and that I will not be. For me not to address that in my work is asking my son to carry that burden.

And, as far as I'm concerned, to the degree that it is possible, this problem ends in my generation. To the degree that I can bring my own work to bear, my own perceptions to bear, to the degree that I can do anything, then I must. And one of my avenues is self-expression. If I believe that art and communication is of value, then I have to step into that breach. And my weapon in that particular fight is my art.

Camille Yarbrough: First, you in your life, as you grow and as you develop, you discover that you are a creative person. All of us have creativity in one area or another. When it comes to the arts, it is a very powerful platform from which to work. When I went into show business, it wasn't because I wanted to go into show business, but that's what was out there. I knew I wanted to be a sharer somehow. And so I went.

At that time, when I was growing up, there wasn't that much opportunity. If you wanted to be a singer, you were limited. If you wanted to be an actress, you were stereotyped again.

And so the easiest road for me, and the one that came to me, was as a dancer. I was lucky enough to be a member of the *Katherine Dunham Dance Company* for five years, and to teach that technique, and to travel the world with that company. And having the experience of working in a cultural setting, which was African at its base, that gave me—that released some energy that was in me and helped to give me a direction.

Later on, when I came back to New York and went on the stage and did some Broadway and off-Broadway and soap operas, I discovered that was not what I wanted. Even though I wanted to be on stage, there was something else that had to be there. Eventually, I discovered that I wanted to communicate, and that I wanted to tell our story.

You are best at telling what you know about, what's closest to you. And being raised on the South Side of Chicago in a family of eight children, visiting relatives from the South, a mother and father and various animals, and being raised in that community which was so rich, is what drew me back to it. And then I found through study and through examination that there are those people called jelis or griots who uphold the culture. That's their job.

I played the *Playboy* club. I'm standing up on the stage singing and I'm saying, "Something's wrong here. This is—it doesn't speak to me." I did other shows. But it just didn't do it. But when I put that aside and began to study our culture and to remember how we related, that is when the light turned on. That's the energy that energizes me. And then in reading, you see that there is in our tradition spiritual specialists brought here from the motherland who worked through the arts. And I find that over the years, that is the category that I fall into. So my work will only reflect things that support our community.

I also was influenced by Paul Robeson, who said—what were the words—"The artist is here to feed the community through the arts." And I feel the response that I'm getting from our community because we need soothing. We need to see visions of ourselves on a different level. We need healing. We need so much. I'm privileged to have been put in that position to do that work. And that's what I reflect.

And so if that answers the questions, there's no contradiction there for me when I work first from home, because you are best at what you know about. And as Lorraine Hansberry said, "If you are specific, you are universal." And so I will be very specifically African, very specifically Black, and the world will be able to see my humanity in that presentation.

Carlos Russell: Carl?

Carl Hancock Rux: I love that the very last thing, the very last word that Nana Yarbrough just said was the word specific.

So, in answer to the question about who our responsibility is to as artists and the communities that we belong to, in this room right now, we're here within a context. We all come together under one context. But we all, I think, as individuals belong to many different communities. And if we look at our lives, we realize how many worlds and communities we belong to. And our responsibility is to all of them.

I am born and raised in New York City. I was raised in the New York City foster care system. My biological mother, who was mentally ill, and institutionalized all of her life, recently died. I was adopted at the age of 15. There was alcoholism in my household. There was spousal abuse in my household. I had an older brother who found me after some years and then died, actually, of AIDS. And I was primary caretaker of the younger brother, who was also raised in foster care all of his life.

So those things became immediate for me; before I ever thought about being a writer or being about anything, I realized that I was a product of an institutionalized system. And I realized that I was a young Black male who basically was a case number and had come from a generation of people who were case numbers, in one way or another; who had received government checks and government funding, and who were living in rooms that were being paid for. The government paid for their care but did not necessarily nurture them, or cultivate them, or move them beyond their circumstance.

So when I decided that I wanted to write, I was responding

to that. I was responding to an investigation. Jane Austen said, "I reserve the right to invade my own privacy." And I decided that that's what I had to do. I had to invade my own privacy. And not just to heal myself, but to really deal with the reality of what was going on in my community, whether some people wanted to hear it or not.

By the way, I should say that my adoptive father and mother were born and raised in Harlem. He was born in 1913. She was born in 1923. So I got the best of history that I could possibly get from two people who had lived through some eras that were beyond me. So many people don't even have the opportunity to talk to their grandparents, no less people who've had access—have access to people who were their parents who had lived through so much. He had fought in World War II. She had been a dancer. They had music in their home. They would sit and have these great conversations about jazz and about jazz music. And all of this became so incredibly important to me because I was inheriting a wealth of information.

So it wasn't just alcoholism and spousal abuse in my home, but there was history in my home. There was pain, but there was joy. There was beauty. There was ugliness. And all of this is me. And all of this is the world and the community that I grew up in. And there were books. And I was able to access so many different things.

I just think that as an artist, I was able to tell that story and continue to investigate and look at that story. But it doesn't stop there. So, who is, what is the community that I'm responsible to: a thousand communities perhaps? I think that I became a little disappointed at a point with some of my friends who would throw around very loosely words like revolution, words like community, words like our people, the cause, the movement.

I became very disappointed because I felt like they were sort of just regurgitating words that they'd heard. And they were emulating in one way or another artists that they respected without really getting into the work of scratching the surface and trying to investigate themselves, and who they were, and what was going on in the rooms that they were living in. And the only time you can really talk to anybody else about what's going on, is if you kind of understand the architecture of your house and you understand the room that you came up in. And you understand that infrastructure and what that was about.

So I didn't concentrate, and I still don't try to concentrate or think about the movement, the struggle because, on one level, it means to me that there is a struggle, and there is a movement, but it may not be the one that I thought.

Carlos Russell: And that is the point, Carl.

Carl Hancock Rux: Yes.

Carlos Russell: In listening to all three of you, Steve said, "We need to know who you are."

Carl Hancock Rux: Right.

Carlos Russell: And my question is, knowing who you are within one context—within what context, the context of the greater Americana or as Camille later talked about referring to her African reality. And you then talked about the question of community and growing up in different sectors of the city as a whole. And you mentioned also the notion of the use of language. Now, if you take all of that with what Steve said at the outset, the notion of the need to survive to live (because you cannot be a revolutionary and don't eat, okay. So you have to take care of that also. If the artist does not eat, then he dies or she dies), the question then, is how do you then merge that, fit that, think it through, so that you are not simply writing to please white America or simply writing to sell, or simply sending a message? What is the message you would like to send?

Carl Hancock Rux: I'm probably the wrong person to ask about writing to sell, because I wrote a novel that's with Simon and Schuster called *Asphalt.* And a lot of my work, whether it's plays or theater or even novels is often not commercial in its way because I'm—it's not what I'm thinking about. It's not how I write or what I need to do. You know what I mean?

Carlos Russell: But when you dance, then?

Carl Hancock Rux: I don't dance, I write for dance and I've collaborated with dancers and dance companies because I think it's important, because I think it helps me as a writer. But I mean, ultimately, I think of what are you doing? Are you committed to yourself or are you trying to sell a product? On one level this involves the level of professionalism. Everybody should figure out how to cultivate themselves and cultivate their craft. Nobody should just jump up and say, "Today I've decided to be a pilot" without ever taking one flying lesson.

It's very important that you kind of begin to think about what you want to do. And then you investigate how it's done. And then you find your voice.

But just one little thing I was going to say is that my last name is Rux, R-U-X, which is a German name. Carl Stephen Rux. My brothers were German. And I began to read a lot about Afro-Germans and I realized that my name is my name because I'm a product of this Afro-German relationship. And after seeing years and years and years of movies about World War II and the Holocaust, and hearing stories and reading books, I kept wondering about the African representation in Europe during that time, as well as the African representation in Germany.

I was looking at some silent films and I saw some Black people dancing around, a 1922 silent film, and I was like, well, who are they? And where were they? And what was going on and what was their story? And there were books and things that people have written recently about the reality, my father having fought in World

War II, about the reality of people of African descent, and how those stories are often not told.

So in investigating my family, I began to investigate our Afro-German history and our Afro-European presence in stories that we are often not exposed to. So this is the book that I'm working on. This is the second novel. It may sell. It may not sell. But the point is that the investigation is the thrust. It is the thing that you have to know. It is finding out something that begins with something you need to know about yourself, and then something you need to know about all of us. And if you don't know it, somebody else in the room doesn't know it. And if you're interested, maybe that will sell, whatever it is.

Carlos Russell: Steve, and then Camille. Your response.

Steven Barnes: You've got a couple of different issues here. For instance, when I said I wanted to be a writer as a child, that meant that I wanted to spend as much of my time as possible writing. There were other things I wanted, too. I also wanted to have a family. I wanted to have a woman that I could love and share with. And I wanted to have children. And that meant I needed to be able to make a living. Now, that meant either I have those two things as separate things or I find a way to put them together. And because I decided that I could learn to be a writer more by writing, even if I was writing commercially, than I would by flipping burgers, I decided that I wanted to learn how to be a commercial artist and then find a way within the realm within commercial art to really express myself. Some of the writers I admired the most over the course of human history had written for food. There's nothing wrong with that part of the struggle. Then it was a matter of, can I find a way to do that dance?

If you gave Fred Astaire a stage of any size and shape, he'd find a way to create art on it. If I understood what the strictures were, what it was that made it possible to create commercial art, what is sales, in other words. What is it that the person on the other side, the audience, going to be willing to exchange their time and energy and money for? I would find the answer. I found that I was not in conflict with the question, how do I best express myself, because I understood that if you go deeply enough into the specific you emerge at the universal.

And then, over the course of learning how to write, I began to move towards the question of who is my audience. And my audience ultimately is me. I write to an audience of me. I write for me. I assume that if I write for my own pleasure, and I write purely for my own pleasure, there are out there in the world enough people who feel like me, and think like me, and are like me enough that if I satisfy myself deeply enough, I will also be satisfying them.

Ultimately it's a yin and yang diagram. There is this set of the things I would like to write, and there is this set of the things I think I can sell. And where those two circles overlap, that's where I write. There's stuff I'd like to write that I don't think I can sell. I'm not going to write it because I cannot afford to spend a year of my life working on something that I cannot make money on. It'd be disastrous.

But on the other hand, there are things that people would love for me to write that I have no interest in. And I won't do that either. I think that if I'm honest enough and if I go deeply enough, what is man that thou art mindful of him? I'm interested in that question. What are we as creatures? What are we in our existence? What is the "illness" of humanity?

Part of that does have to do with race and culture and gender and all kinds of things like that. And there's all sorts of room for wonderful conflict, and commercial fiction is built on conflict. Stuff happens; people respond to it; people have goals and dreams and hopes. How people react within the landscape of the world that you're creating is the fuel, the emotions that people are experiencing within that story, the combustibles. That's the dynamite. That's the gunpowder. And you stamp it down into this package that has to do with universals of human experience, which is what the hero's journey is.

You have somebody who wants something and they face their fear with wanting it. And they commit to going after it. And they set out on the road of trials during which they meet allies and gain powers and they fail. And they have to deal with their failure, and they have to find some way to have faith. These are stories that have been told over and over again throughout all of human history. And if I structure that and if I'm always finding a way to tell the truth within that, then no matter how trivial the commercial package is and believe me, some of the stuff I've done has had very trivial commercial packaging, I mean, I wrote four episodes of *Baywatch*. It pays the bills, what can I say?

But even there, I was able to say something that I thought was true about the nature of human relationships. I was able to say that a relationship isn't two people looking at each other; it's two people looking in the same direction. And just that moment of truth, I was able to put in front of a billion people worldwide. And that was meaningful to me.

Carlos Russell: Camille?

Camille Yarbrough: Yes. I had a couple of relationships with writers who had gone before, and who told me certain things, reassuring things that I had myself lived with. I had the acquaintance of a writer named Alice Childress, a recent ancestor. Oh, God, thank you for that. She told me many stories because she had been before me, and she was telling me things. And then I'd heard it also when I did the play *To Be Young, Gifted and Black* by Lorraine Hansberry.

Both of them had written plays. I think it was Alice Childress who wrote a screenplay. She had been asked to write it for television on Nat Turner. Lorraine Hansberry had been asked to write a play on Fanny Lou Hamer for television. They wrote it. They put it in. Got paid. But it was never shown.

Recently, one of our big actresses right now, a very successful actress who recently won an Academy, some years ago, read the story of Ida B. Wells. And she expressed her desire to do that. She was approached by one of our very, very high-placed producers, a woman sister who came to her and said, "Don't do that. Don't do that. That'll just get you into trouble. We have a biography we would like you to do." And she ended up doing a biography of a performer, which had not the impact or the importance of the story of Ida B. Wells and what it would have meant to us.

We have to face the fact of that word racism, which we've been told doesn't exist anymore. It exists. We've been told that it does not affect us. It affects our lives. I cannot write, and I will not write to entertain white people or to support them. There are some good white people out here. But the system is wrong. The system is belittling us. The system is undercutting us all the time. And we as artists must stand up and face it and talk it down, the way we did before, the way we did some years ago. It was Nina Simone who got up and said "Mississippi god damn." It was other artists who said, "What's going on, a little respect. When will we be paid for the work we've done?"

And they went on and on because the movement was there and the artists helped it. Mahalia Jackson got up and sang in support of Dr. King. Yes, she got paid, but she got up there and she sang. And many artists, we do not know. We don't remember what happened to Aretha when she was standing up. A lot of artists went through changes, had their careers stopped, had nervous breakdowns where lives were threatened because they were telling our story in a way that this system did not want it to be told.

What did Harriet Tubman say when she traveled from the South from the plantations up into Canada? She was asked, "Whatcha gonna do now?" She said, "I'm gonna start it all over." And it's time for us to start it all over. Look how our artists are being misused against us. I have a magazine, which I was showing to the sister who works with me. On the cover was Little Kim. She looked like a schoolgirl. Then inside was a story of Little Kim. Well, look at Little Kim now. Look at what has happened to her in this system. Look at what has happened to a lot of our sisters and brothers in this system.

How is it that now we're calling ourselves the kind of names we're calling each other and the disrespect? The artist is being used as the agent of change to reintroduce things that we had forgotten, reintroduce things we had overcome. And we have to stand up and stop it. And we have to do it now, people.

You travel to Europe. You travel around the world. Who was it? It was a sister who got all that money, got that radio program, television program. You know, Oprah, who recently went into South Africa and somebody addressed her, "Hi nigger." And then other people are now going around the country saying, "Hey, nigger." What is this?

Our young people use it because they don't know where that word came from. And it's been given to them just like some Eddie Murphy when he was on television; he came back with the, what's that, the big 'fro?

Carlos Russell: Buckwheat.

Camille Yarbrough: Buckwheat. Where did that 'fro come from? Why was it necessary for us to let our hair grow like that? What's the story behind the 'fro? I remember when I stopped straightening my hair and what a job it was to get to that place where I stood in front of the mirror and said, "No, I'm not going to do this anymore." What did Maulana Karenga say? "Define your self." And we have stopped defining our selves. We are going along with the going along to get along.

And I'm saying, right now, we are in a dangerous condition. Right now, what's happening to us here and around the world? Why is it that people are being slaughtered in Africa by other people who look like us, Africans, and nobody's saying a word? If this were in the 1960s, we'd be up. We'd be marching. We'd be doing something. We'd be in somebody's office. But right now, we just sit down, look, and turn to another channel. Uh-huh. What has happened to us people? Please forgive me, but I think we're in a dangerous situation here, and we better wake up. And we'd better do something about it.

I look at our children, how they're growing up in this world of disrespect. We would never tolerate that when we were young. You know what your parents said to you. You know how your parents raised you. There are certain things you didn't say, certain things you didn't do out of respect, not because you were afraid. And how many times have I been told by young people, "It's your fault. It's the elder's fault that we're in this trouble because you didn't do what you were supposed to do."

Well, I know people who gave their lives. I know a lot of people who gave up their careers, gave up their education to raise their children to stop the racism in this country. And then they did a pre-emptive strike. They went past us because they did not want this generation to do what the previous generation had done: burned this country down almost and stopped the racism. They did not want this new generation to do it. And so they went to them. They separated them from the elders, told them that elders didn't like them. Told them that elders were not going to support them, built up dissention between them.

And then they fed them, through the genius of our young people to create that which we call hip-hop. It was a genius creation at the beginning. But look at it now. Look at it now. Look at what the system has done to it now. Look what the system has done to our people. You look at the young brothers walking down with their jailhouse pants on. You see the brothers walking down the street and they surreptitiously pull them up on the side. But their mind says, "That's where they have to be."

Carlos Russell: Thank you, Camille.

Camille Yarbrough: I'm sorry. That's the way it is.

Carlos Russell: I believe that the passion that you have just heard expressed in Camille's retort and response is an indication why the question that began this panel is so important. Because what it underscores is that the artist then must create the images and send the symbols that we want our youngsters to emulate. The difficulty as it appears, is that presently we still depend on the larger society to publish, to promote the works that we do, which is in a sense a contradiction because John Henrik Clarke once said that the slave cannot expect to get his freedom by copying the cultural incubator of his oppressor. And if you listen to that, you can see that we find ourselves in difficulties. And I think some of the difficulties have been expressed very clearly when Steve, for example, says that he had to write four chapters for *Baywatch*, was it? Yet *Baywatch* reached millions of people. And look at what you're seeing presently on the television. What you are seeing I would call nothing more than buffoonery. There are no *The Man Who Cried I Am*, and so forth and so on.

And for you, my brother, I just add that—and I'm sure you know, but I just add, Carl, that Namibia and South Africa were controlled, as you know, by the Germans. And people talk about the German Holocaust. But in the German Holocaust, it was not only Jews, it was Black folks from Namibia.

Camille Yarbrough: That's right. That's right. And Cameroon.

Carlos Russell: I want to shift slightly now back to another reality that we have to deal with. Each and every one of you functions on many different levels. You are dancers, novelists, and writers for television, songs, and etcetera. There are some people who will say that your artistry is reduced if you stay solely within one category, one area. But we are finding today that there is much more of a blurring of the areas. Where do you come out in that? How do you do it? Is it a difficulty for you to be able to deal with the blurring of the many different areas of your artistry? Or do you think that is much more helpful to us since our communities across the board are much more diverse in terms of their interests?

Carl Hancock Rux: I'll just say that I've been asked a lot, "Oh, you write novels and you write poetry and you write plays and work with theater people, you work in dance," as if this were new. And it's not. I mean, Maya Angelou was a poet and a playwright and screenwriter and a novelist and a singer and a dancer and a director. Langston Hughes was a poet and a memoirist and essayist and a novelist and—I just feel like this is—we've been doing this forever.

It's all about the permission you give yourself. I feel like I'm a writer, period. And then whatever, however the muse speaks to me, whether the muse that day says, "There's a thought that you need to express but this isn't novel length. This is one poem and it needs to be about two stanzas. Say it and get it over with." And that's what I have to obey. And if the muse says that "you don't know, you actually have 300 pages of something that you have to investigate and you need to deal with." And I'll just do that.

I'll work with dancers because I don't think that you can understand words unless you start to understand how words are expressed non-verbally and unless you understand what's actually happening in the body.

Some of the greatest writers I've ever seen or read were people who didn't work within a publishing medium, but were people who choreographed and people who danced. And Katherine Dunham's greatest essays were what she did on stage. And I learned so much from looking at those video clips, and her going to Haiti and her bringing that work back. So I really feel like it was necessary to work with dance, and work with music, and in all forms.

So, what's usually said to me is that art is reduced if you work as a multi-disciplinary artist. People usually think that if you're spreading yourself so thin, then you can't really be a writer, you must not really be a musician, you're not really a playwright, whatever, if you're doing all of those things at the same time. And I just think that that's a lie. And we've always done this. And it's not new. We've always danced. We've always sung. We've always written poems. We've always done exactly what I'm doing.

We've just come to a period in time where people have decided to commercialize and marginalize and relegate you to a form and say, "This is what you're supposed to do. And this is how you're supposed to do it. And you're not supposed to combine it or mess it up or mix it up with anything else."

And that's another lie. And it's a lie that I had to reject in the universities and that I continue to reject.

Carlos Russell: Steve, or anyone.

Steven Barnes: Okay, I would say that excellence is simply excellence. I mean that the primary job of a human being is to be an excellent human being. There are three different arenas in which I try to express myself, and only one of them is what other people refer to as the arts. Within that, then there is this question of, once again, who am I? What is it that I really think and feel? What really appeals to me aesthetically and whether I'm shaping, regardless of what it is that I'm shaping, it's that aesthetic sense. And that's like water. And this water can be poured into a number of different types of containers. And it can be steam or it can be ice. Or it can be in a jug. It can be moving. It can be still. But the water is the artistic urge.

And whether it's a poem or whether it's a play. I've written 20 novels. I've written short stories. I've written for television. I've written magazine articles. I've been on the radio. I've done film. I've done this. I've done that. And it all starts in the exact same place. If I were to be confused to think that each of these different things is something completely different, then I can see why somebody could make that mistake.

I think that people speak to their own limitations when they say, "Well, why don't you spend all your time doing one thing." Well, yes, you can spend all your time doing one thing, learning about one thing. But you learn a lot about the world by seeing how it's done someplace else.

How does a farmer make a living? You learn about life there. How does a shoemaker make a shoe? You learn about writing a novel there. How does a mother raise child? Understanding how a poet does his or her work, how a dancer does what a dancer does, how someone working with metal does that, and then, by understanding these things, then you ask yourself what is the same about all of this, because every individual project is something new.

Every day is both exactly the same as other days and completely unique. And you shouldn't make the mistake of thinking that each individual form is something separate, rather than a different branch that has the same roots. Be observant, and willing to tell the truth, and willing to work your ass off, and willing to deal with fear, and willing to deal with pain, and willing to go into the places inside yourself that society tells you, don't look at feeling. Don't look at what is unique about you. Instead of that, just take the symbols that we have given you and regurgitate them. And we will give you money for this. If you will go into the places that are uniquely you, if you will look at your pain, if you will look at the disowned parts of yourself, the places that are forbidden to go to, that is where you will find the roots of your own individual expression.

Okay? And it's through that that you have prayer of giving to the world something that it has not seen.

Carlos Russell: Camille.

Camille Yarbrough: When I was employed at City College there was something that we observed with the students. When we told them that the major religions had started on the continent of Africa and were created by Africans, and that people took this from them and created their own, students didn't believe it. When we told them the major sciences, the basic, the foundations started in ancient Kush and the Sudan area, and Ethiopia, and were spread around the world, they didn't believe that either. It had to be proven to them. And then they still had an attitude of not believing this about Black folk. We are a gifted people. I'm not saying this for feel good reasons.

We are very gifted people. And we're not used to hearing it or knowing it. I'm not talking feel good to you. I'm saying just when you acknowledge who you are, then you know that you can do a plethora of things.

Tyler Perry in this new film he's put out. What is it, *Madea's Family Reunion?* The man is an actor. He acts many parts. He is a composer. He wrote it. He directed it. That's an example of one person who has done many things. We have a lot of that with our people, but we don't know it. And so I'm saying, it is easy for us to do many things. This society says, "You all can't do it." But why? "You can't do nothing. You're always talking about race. You all can't do this. You all can't." We can do it. We can do it all. But they were not hiring us to do it. The thing is to get us to stop focusing on ourselves and start telling somebody else's story.

When I did the soap opera *Search for Tomorrow*, a lot of us auditioned because there were no Blacks on those shows except one sister, Ellen Holly, who was very light-skinned. I auditioned. This was during the movement. We had moved this country. We went into the colleges, into the hotels and motels around the country. We could get in now. We did that. We changed this country. And I was naïve enough to think that when we went on soap operas, we'd be able to tell our story.

When I got on the soap opera, they said, "No, it's not about racism. It's because you're a woman that you were not given that." Well, the women's movement was righteous, but it did not bring us to where we are. The movement did it.

Carlos Russell: Thank you, Camille. Thank you. I want to go to the audience now and to keep the promise that I said that you would get an opportunity to ask questions and to interact with the panel.

Male Speaker: Hi, my name is Carlos Greer and I want to first thank all of you for such an informative panel, and for the way that it was actually formatted. I thought it was really important to really pose the question of what's our responsibility to our people. Ms. Yarbrough, thank you for acknowledging artists being misused against us.

I have a quick story. A few years ago, I was in a classroom taking a writing-for-television class where one of the assignments was to write an episode to an existing show. And one white student, decided to write an episode to the show *The Office*. And basically, in her episode, she wanted the cast in *The Office,* to come dressed as their favorite celebrity. And for one of the characters, she wanted his favorite celebrity to be Samuel L. Jackson. And so I posed a question: How are you going to write this? And is it going to require a black face, which it would. And the class thought it was hysterical. They all laughed, even the Black students in this class. And one white student was like, well, Dave Chappelle did it. Dave Chappelle does it. And they all jumped down my throat. And I was like the angry Black man in this class.

But it really made me think about in the last panel where they quoted Martin Luther King saying that we're integrating ourselves into a burning house. The question is basically, how do we, as artists and as writers, not only think about "the mainstream"? How do we bring our stories outside of the university? How do we bring it to East St. Louis where I'm from for example? How do we bring our stories outside of academia? When we're on our book signings, how do we take it outside of these little coffee shops and book houses and bring it to the community?

Steven Barnes: Okay. As it happens, *Madea's Family Reunion* was brought up. And as it happens, I know as a friend and as a business partner Blair Underwood, who was in it. And we had an opportunity to talk with Blair, who was in the process of creating something called *The Momentum Experience*, where basically what's happening is people are financing film projects using a model that's very similar to what Tyler Perry did. In other words, it's possible to go the Hollywood route. And it's also possible to go outside that, to bring together business people to create small experiences, move them around to different communities that will support these things, and make a perfectly good living. I mean, make perfectly good money doing that. There are lots of different ways to do this.

And what we need is everybody to understand that if you have a dream and you have a vision, and you're willing to tell the truth in your work, which once again is going to be the only way you're ever going to get good, that you can get together with other people who have business experience. If *The Momentum Experience* works, it means the creation of small movies that cost a million, $2 million dollars and then rolling them out across the country to Black communities and then using that to promote the DVD sales. And DVD sales allow you to target very much more precisely. So the entire model of how these things happen is starting to change right underneath Hollywood. It's being taken away from them. Okay? So there's a lot of potential out there. And you're young enough to get on the beginning of that wave. Study the business model that is happening with things like that. You'll see a lot of potential.

Carlos Russell: I will take another question.

Female Speaker: Hello. My name is Danielle Haynes. And I'm originally from Denver, Colorado, but I'm a student at North Carolina Central University majoring in Elementary Education. And my comment is to Miss Camille. It's in regards to when you were talking about the younger generation and with the Little Kim situation. And I just wanted to stand up and say that I think that my generation is fully aware of the choices that they make. Usually, in life you have two choices; one choice is to either do or the other choice is to either not do. And in the Little Kim situation, she had a choice. And she lied. And that didn't have anything to do

145

necessarily with the system. But she lied to the law system. And so that, I feel, is not necessarily the best example for that.

And then also I wanted to say a comment about the generation. I just wanted to talk about how you said the younger generation blames the older generation for the things that we go through now. I don't feel that that necessarily is true, because I do know a lot of students who are my age, and who are younger, who do appreciate the things that people before us have done, and the places that they have made able for us to be, as in college and different places. So I just wanted to come up here and say that. Thank you.

Carlos Russell: Thank you.

Camille Yarbrough: Okay. So, concerning Little Kim. I wasn't speaking of that last episode of the shooting, and where she said that she didn't see anybody and that thing. I was speaking of her as a beginning artist, what she looked like, how she carried and presented herself as a beginning artist. And then what happened to her. The medium sculpts you. She came up in Brooklyn in a section of the city, which was rough. Many of us did and she came up with Biggie. And so when those with the money came and they told her to change the color of hair, to change what you wear, she said, "Okay, I'll go along with that." That's what I'm saying. She went along with things that this system destroys.

I want you to look at it with me, that tremendous voice that woman had. I'm saying that the system is destructive.

Just one more thing, what else did—oh, I only said that the elders are being separated, and the young people are saying that they don't trust the elders. Many of them have said this to me. Many artists, hip-hop artists, have pointed their finger at a sister who has an organization in the Bronx, and told her that it's your fault that we are in the trouble that we're in. Kanye West, whom I respect on one level, in one of his DVDs stands up and says, "Well, I used to talk good about the Africans, but now I know that they sold us. So I'm not going to talk good about them anymore." He's believing the hype, believing the lie. And it's our responsibility, some of us sold us, some of us in America are selling each other, ain't never been to Africa. So we have to—we have to share.

You, my child, do you understand? We are family. That's why I wear this hat. That's why I wrote that song, "Family Forever, family forever, don't let anything come between us."

Carl Hancock Rux: I think that I was glad that you said what you said. And understanding everybody of the hip-hop generation is not in agreement. There's always this idea that everybody who's from a certain generation actually believes and follows along with, and agrees with everything that comes out. And that's certainly not true and it's certainly not what Nana Yarbrough was saying.

But I was just going to say very quickly that there are two things. One is I think what was really being said is how easy it is to get lost in an industry and to lose yourself. I interviewed Little Kim for *Interview* magazine. And I'll never forget the interview because as we were talking, it was kind of a difficult conversation. But at the end of it, I said to her, "What do you want? What do you want from your career? What do you want for the rest of your life now as an artist? What are you looking forward to?" And she said, "I want to be like Michael Jackson."

And I'll never forget how sad it made me when she said it. I actually teared up a little bit. Because I kept thinking, do you know what you've just said? And she said, "You know." And I said, "Why do you want to be like Michael Jackson?" And she said, "You know, he has his own house and he has all that land. And he's got the animals. And he's got power. And he can just do whatever he wants. And I love that. And it's beautiful. And I want that."

And this is at a point when I think she couldn't see what Michael Jackson was going through. There's that sort of surface thing, and it scared me when she said it because I thought, "Gee, how could you not see yourself wanting your own demise? How could you not hear yourself wanting your own demise?" And it was sort of interesting.

The other thing I was going to say very quickly is about being lost in the industry. I love that this sister ran up to me on the street the other day and she said, "You know, Carl, what is this movie they got out now? What's the title of it, *Get Rich or Die Trying?*" And then she just kept screaming. And she was like, "what is that, *Get Rich or Die Trying?*" Like why, and how could 50 Cent make a movie like that. Here we are in the top of our game, the hip-hop generation and this is our big opportunity, big stance. Fine, it's a movie. It's out. It's commercial. But the title alone was already dangerous. And so it was already a dangerous message. It was already a dangerous thing that was being said.

So whether we believe it or not or buy into every little thing, there are things that are said that we're not aware that we're saying. And not really aware of how damaging it is.

Male Speaker: I am a high school teacher in my second year. And well, first of all, yes, just thank you. This has been a very valuable panel discussion. I didn't think it would go all the way to the subject of the change, all the way up to the subject of what we have to do. But my question is, as a high school teacher, I have to say my kids don't know what's happening. They don't even understand that there needs to be any kind of a change. And my question is, knowing that my kids are going to be so real, that they're not going to do anything without understanding why, how is it that maybe young people can understand more why and understand better why there needs to be a change? Why things need to change in terms of what they're seeing and how they're reacting to it?

Carlos Russell: The answer is very simple. If you do not want to change, you will remain in jail. And incarceration within this society sends so many different messages, and keeps us from realizing our potential as an African people. This will destroy you.

And as Carl said, "We should not participate in our own decimation." And the roles that teachers have are to explain clearly to their students that there is a contradiction between what the society says and the reality that is their lives.

Male Speaker: Yes. I understand.

Camille Yarbrough: There's a teacher right now who is almost in court because she tried to teach African Studies, or give the children an idea of their heritage. She is under attack. She's been suspended. She also found one of the young children put in a cage in the gym. And she was suspended for that. When we try, my brother man, you are the teacher. You are in there. And I know there are pressures on you. I've worked with other teachers. Some of the teachers close the door and teach what they should teach.

Carlos Russell: Exactly.

Camille Yarbrough: But other teachers find it very difficult to teach anything that's not in the curriculum. And there's this Underground Railroad curriculum.

Carlos Russell: Yes. There is a curriculum that supposed to teach that.

Camille Yarbrough: Yes. The teachers are supposed to teach, but they're not teaching it because they're under pressure not to teach it. We have to get in those schools. Remember the Ocean Hill—Brownsville fight? We got to do it over again, just like Harriet said. Help the teachers. The teachers in there are trying to do the best they can, but the community is separated from the school. How is that going to work?

Carlos Russell: I agree.

Female Speaker: This is to Carl or Steven. You discussed telling the truth. And you were just talking about an African identity, an African awareness, and the strength in our children. And I just want to address the inside of what the evolution is because there's also a spiritual evolution. Is my spiritual self expressed through art or whatever form that is?

Steven Barnes: See, to me, the spirit can't be addressed directly. It can be addressed indirectly. Like grass bending is not the wind. But you can see the wind in the bending of the grass. You look at the things that are of this world. And I say that the three things you look at is your relationship to your family and the people around you, especially your significant other; your relationship to your body, which is your vehicle through this world and the respect that you have for it and the way you take care of it; and your contribution to your community, the way you make your way in terms of your career, the goods and services that you create and the self respect that demands that the community respond to you. That if you look at those three things, spirit is in the middle of that triangle. And then whatever spiritual tradition that you follow, look at the way it influences those three things and you will never go wrong.

Carlos Russell: Thank you. I want to wrap up and I want to use Steve's last words as a key. A prime element within the African tradition has always been spirit. We are spirit people. And the reality is, "we are family forever," as my good friend Nana Yarborough constantly reminds me. And she also reminds me of the notion that we have to listen to our ancestors and the spirits that have kept us together.

CHAPTER EIGHT

Reflections On The
Creative Writing Process

Valerie Wilson Wesley
interviewed by Richard Wesley

Richard Wesley: I have known Valerie since she was 19 years old. We were college classmates together in a Philosophy and Logic class at Howard University. She was much better at it than I was— am. We have, in one way or another, been together ever since. We've been friends and we've been married for 35 years.

Valerie Wilson Wesley is the author of *Playing My Mother's Blues*, which is her latest novel, and other novels include, my favorite, *Ain't Nobody's Business If I Do*. That was followed by *Always True to You in My Fashion*. Then there are the Tamara Hayle mysteries, for which I think she may be most well known. Sometimes when I read these titles here, it seems like Val is trying to tell the family something. The first novel was *When Death Comes Stealing*. It was followed by *The Devil Is Going to Get Her, Where Evil Sleeps, No Hiding Place, Easier to Kill, The Devil Riding,* and *Dying In the Dark*.

She's also written a series of books for children. *Willimena Rules* is the name of the series, and the first four books in the series are *Rule Book Number One: How To Lose Your Class Pet, Rule Book Number Two: How to Fish for Trouble, Rule Book Number Three: How to Lose Your Cookie Money, and Rule Book Number Four: 23 Ways to Mess Up Valentine's Day.* Somehow I have a feeling that fourth book was meant for me. Another book was a young adult novel. It's out of print, but it also happens to be, again, a little special for me, because I believe this one, *Freedom's Gifts, A Juneteenth Story,* was the first story that Valerie wrote that I ever read. She showed me the original manuscript of it and I'm hoping somehow, some way we—

Valerie Wilson Wesley: He's wrong. Richard, leave it alone. You got it wrong. [Laughter] We'll talk about that later.

Richard Wesley: It is. This is the story.

Valerie Wilson Wesley: No, no, no. Go ahead. Go ahead. Go ahead. [Laughter] Just maybe get to the questions.

Richard Wesley: Okay, *Easier To Kill.*

Valerie Wilson Wesley: Thank you, sweetheart. That's fine.

Richard Wesley: So Valerie, where do your characters come from?

Valerie Wilson Wesley: Maybe I shouldn't respond to that. No. My husband, first of all, I just want to say a few words of introduction because he's very modest. My husband is a screenwriter. His films include *Uptown Saturday Night, Let's Do It Again, Mandela and De Klerk* and *Amazing Deacons for Defense,* which was on Showtime. His plays include *The Black Terror, The Mighty Gents,* and *The Talented Tenth.* He is an amazing screenwriter and an amazing playwright and he's fantastic, and he's a great guy.

Being married as writers, people often ask, "Are you competitive?" No, because he's writing for film and for television and I'm writing novels. And they're completely different ways to write. I think in terms of our characters; they probably come from the same place in the sense that characters are always a combination of many different people. You don't really lift a character. You don't say, "Well, I'm going to base this character on this person or that person." But little tiny bits of people, little tiny bits of things that you know about a person, trying to get the inner thing of a person, the inner essence of a person is how I create my characters. I guess it's similar for you. You never lift something straight out from reality.

Richard Wesley: When you are writing, though, do you see a physical representation of these characters in your mind?

Valerie Wilson Wesley: Yes, absolutely. I think that's, in some ways, how it's similar to film. I know that if Tamara Hayle were to walk into this room, or my latest characters in *Playing My Mother's Blues,* I would know immediately who they were, because you have to know the character that well in order to create her or him. That's essential. What's essential to writing well is knowing your character, every part of them: the way they talk, what they wear, where they were born, things that don't come into the novel.

Richard Wesley: Well, sometimes when you get up from your computer and you go take care of something else in the house, and you leave the computer on, I peek at some of the things that—

Valerie Wilson Wesley: I suspected as much.

Richard Wesley: But the one thing I always noticed, I see you outlining the novel and everything, but I often wonder, do you write out bios for your characters?

Valerie Wilson Wesley: I do, but not until I actually write out a couple of lines of dialogue and then I can hear the character's voice, and I know that character better, and that's really essential for me. I suspect for you as a screenwriter it's a similar kind of thing.

Richard Wesley: So you create this internal bio when you are actually writing the story. Do you find yourself wanting to change some things because the characters themselves have surprised you in some way?

Valerie Wilson Wesley: There is always a certain element of surprise for me as a writer. I don't know about you. Very often— if you're writing a novel or a short story—you get a block. Very often it's because the character wouldn't do what you thought in your mind when you set out that they were going to do. But the more that you've written the character and the more you know the character, then you realize that they would go into a different direction. I think sometimes writing is a combination of craft, but it's also a certain magic. And that is what is essential for me.

Richard Wesley: I think at one time you had one of these surprises force you to change the direction of the story.

Valerie Wilson Wesley: It often happens. Even in *Playing My Mother's Blues*, which I'm going to read from this evening.

Richard Wesley: Then which comes first, the story or the character? Do you tend to think out—like for instance, you get an idea. Is the idea story-inspired or is the idea character-inspired, or is it just depending on the circumstances?

Valerie Wilson Wesley: I think it's a combination of both for me. Sometimes it depends upon the genre I'm writing in. I write mysteries. I write children's books. I write novels. It really depends. Mysteries are always plot-driven. There is one character, in my case, Tamara Hayle. It's always the same person, same voice: first person, singular. Same setting: Newark, for the most part. It's a mystery. So you know you have certain things that you must lay out in a mystery. You have to have red herrings. You have to have a murder, or it wouldn't be a mystery. You know by the end of the piece, the murder must be solved. There are clues that must come into a mystery. That's an essential part of a mystery. Nobody wants to read a mystery where there are no clues, because the fun of reading the mystery is being able to see can I outwit the writer with this? And often you all do with me.

So basically, in that case, it's story, because I already have the characters. But with the novel, it's a kind of a different exercise. I feel the characters more intensely because they change with each novel, and that's the reality of writing novels. That's one reason that I enjoy writing them so much.

Richard Wesley: Now you've written novels, mystery novels, children's books and young adult books. Do you have a preference in terms of a favorite arena that you like to go into as a writer, or is it a situation where whatever the idea is, you move in that particular area?

Valerie Wilson Wesley: I'm working on a Willimena book now, which are always fun because Willimena's my children's character. It's very simple. Her life dilemmas revolve around the guinea pig running away and her needing to explain to the rest of the class how she lost it, or small things, manageable ones. Tamara's life, which is my detective, is much more complex. It's a much more brutal, violent life, and the novels, depending on what I'm writing, can vary as well.

I think in terms of challenging and growing as a writer, my favorite thing is to write novels. It's because it gives me a chance to explore, to go in a different direction. Each novel presents a particular problem. Each one is a particular challenge. Each one, in its own way, is exciting, and so ultimately, that's what I enjoy doing most, are the novels. I love it, but then on the other hand, coming back to Tamara Hayle, after an absence of four years, it was great. It was like hanging out with a good friend. So it really pretty much depends. I kind of enjoy them all.

Richard Wesley: I guess I ask that question because of the way the publishing industry is, the way the entertainment industry is now. Writers are expected to be specialists. There is the writer who only writes comedy. There's the writer who only writes action-adventure in screen; and in the area of publishing, one has always expected if you've established a reputation for yourself as a mystery novelist, that's what you're always going to write, so why do you want to bust out in so many directions?

Valerie Wilson Wesley: I think the publishers asked that too. I ended up working for three different publishers. My mysteries are out of one publisher. The novel is from another and the children's books are published by yet another, because they really like you to stay where you are, and as a writer, I have to control who I am. I have to control my work. I have to do what means the most for me, and that's one reason I tend to write different things. I have to constantly grow as a writer, constantly hone my skills, and that's what's essential to me.

However, I think in many ways, you sometimes are penalized. People get annoyed when you've done a series and they want you to do something else, but for me it's always about, as a writer, learning and always growing.

Richard Wesley: Is that the advice that you would give to a new writer, someone who is just beginning their career, to think more in terms of having that kind of broad approach to writing, in other words, don't pigeonhole yourself? Don't get stuck in just one particular genre or one particular vein?

Valerie Wilson Wesley: I think good writing is always good writing, no matter what you're working on. And it's very important that you learn your skills, that you learn to do the best writing you can, no matter what you're writing for, or who you're writing for. If you're writing for children, make it the very best children's book that it can be. If you're writing a mystery, really learn the skills, really learn the style and really understand what you're trying to do, and have respect for the craft.

My goodness, I sit down at my computer sometimes after reading a book by Toni Morrison or the writer of that marvelous book, *The Known World,* Edward P. Jones, and it's like, "How dare I turn on my computer?" But the reality is that you pay your respects, in a sense, to these writers and the tradition of writers, because we—as I think we've talked a lot about in this conference—need to understand the importance of controlling our own image, of empowering ourselves by giving that image to our readers.

In other forms, there is always something between. In screenwriting, there is the director; there is the producer. But in writing a novel, it's just us—it's the writer and the reader. From my heart to your ears, I guess you could say. This is what is important. There is that link, so I know that is an essential part of what I do, and you have to respect that.

Richard Wesley: Maybe that explains why so many screenwriters are also experiencing the desire to write novels, to move into that particular area.

Valerie Wilson Wesley: Yes, I think that could be it. You prefer to write plays to screenplays, because it's you to the audience.

Richard Wesley: Yes, I like that centrality. That control. Power.

Valerie Wilson Wesley: That sounds a little weird, doesn't it? That's okay. Leave it alone, sweetheart. [Laughter] That's all right. That's all right.

Richard Wesley: I was just going to ask you, I noticed you write so well about wounded souls, men who are consumed by rage, women whose rebellion is tinged with melancholy, and I wondered do you find yourself saying something specific about life and class in Black America, or are your stories about people who happen to be Black?

Valerie Wilson Wesley: I can only write from what I know. I can only write from the perspective of a woman in her 50s, a mother with two daughters, who has been married 35 years to the same guy, and from the perspective of what I know. I'm a Black woman, so naturally I write about that. I don't say, "Well, I'm just going to write about this life or that." But my books are about color and class more than anything else. They are also about lust and passion, and what happens when we follow passion that is not always well thought out.

It's also about mothers and daughters. It's the first time I've really written about mothers and daughters. It's taken me a long time, because my daughters are now in their 30s. I feel that I have enough distance between raising them to be able to look at the relationship with a certain amount of objectivity and see it with my own mother who passed away about 15 years ago. To answer your question, Rich, I think it's about all of these things. That was a good question.

Richard Wesley: I will open the questions to the audience now.

Female Speaker: It's interesting that you're talking about a story where there are two sisters. I wonder, how do you discipline yourself to keep their personalities so clearly defined, especially when you're talking about two women raised by the same mother, living with the same father, who are obviously going to be different, but in your writing, how do you keep them separate?

Valerie Wilson Wesley: Again, it's going back to character. Really understanding the character, and understanding the impact of what happened. What the mother did, of course, remember the girls were 7 and 17, which is 10 years' difference, in leaving them as she did and killing her lover like she did, had very different impacts on both young women. Rose is in her 40s and Danny is in her 30s when the book takes place. They've grown in a different way. It was complex in that way. I had to really understand these characters very, very well, and I hope that I did. I've been told— many readers have told me that they thought I did a good job. I'll leave it up to you all if you read the book to decide. But again, it's hard. It's hearing the voice. It's knowing the character. The fact that all four voices were in first person made it difficult too, because they really do have a different rhythm, each woman. I thought the book was about Danny. The editor did too, because when you read the flap it mentions Danny. But as I wrote it, I realized the book was actually Mariah's book. She's closer in age to me, and I think that was a natural voice for this story to take place. I hope that answers your question. Thank you.

Female Speaker: Thanks so much, Valerie, for writing over the years. I've been reading your work and teaching it for many, many years. My question is about language. Where were you born? Do you have a Southern ear, or were you born up in the North? That kind of thing, and how that influences how you write, please.

Valerie Wilson Wesley: Okay, I was born actually in Connecticut. I'm an Army brat, as they're called. So I grew up in different countries. I grew up in Madrid, Spain. I was in Germany for four years, and then I went to Howard during the 1960s, which was an amazing time to go. I was kind of a lonely child. I loved to write. I loved to read, and I think being the only Black child in a predominately white environment had a profound impact on me as a youngster. I'm going to write about that at some point. It's very painful, but for writers, a lot of what they write about comes from anguish, early anguish. That is mine, always being different, always being the one who didn't fit. Always feeling out of place. As you grow, I think you take that as a writer.

In terms of growing up as a teenager, because of the very fact that I didn't have any television—everything was in Spanish and German. I just read. What else do you do if you have that problem with TV? I just read voraciously as a teenager. I think that, more than anything else, really pushed me into wanting to become a writer.

Female Speaker: I came in a little bit late, so I don't know if you already touched on this, but if you could speak a little bit about your writing for children, the Willimena series and how you came about to write that. Why you think it was important for you to do that, because you were doing adult novels, mystery novels, and Willimena is a very different form for you.

Valerie Wilson Wesley: (Introducing speaker) This is my very talented young editor, Sahara Faceda, who has a marvelous book out herself. I want to say, first of all, I think Willimena is the first and the only, at this point, young Black girl who is featured in a chapter book. For me, Willimena is a combination of my youngest daughter, Nandi, a little bit of me and a little bit of what I know about childhood.

I used to be a teacher, so I know a bit about children and about growing up. Some people have compared Willimena's spirit in some ways to Tamara Hayle because she is a very smart and very spunky little character. But there is always a moral dilemma she is dealing with, and it's funny because going into this new area, (and I'm working on a new Willimena now) has given me a chance to explore an aspect of me as that 6-year-old, 7-year-old, 8-year-old—and Willimena is around seven or eight—that part of me that still loves to know and loves to experiment, and loves to discover the world. Another thing I get is such marvelous e-mail from children and parents who have really enjoyed the series. That's one reason that I like to write it.

They've been fun. They've been absolute fun to write, and at first I didn't think they would be because I've been writing for adults, but Willimena's world is very safe, and the dilemmas are major for her, as they are for all children. And there are also moral decisions that Willimena makes that often are quite similar to what we as adults make.

Sahara Faceda: You do such a wonderful job with it because it's for young people, and not many writers can do that. Thank you.

Valerie Wilson Wesley: Thank you. It is interesting. It is a bit of a stretch, and I must say, it's frankly, a relief writing them. After Delia, you can imagine what I was after these women. So, Willimena, Willimena, where are you? Tamara's world is quite violent sometimes, and you're dealing with violence and ugly people and mean people and people who murder and do all kinds of stuff. And frankly, coming into a world where one of the more serious things that can happen to you is that you send yourself too many Valentine's Day cards and are embarrassed, is quite nice. So I enjoy. Thanks for asking that.

Richard Wesley: We have time for one more question.

Valerie Wilson Wesley: Just one? I'm enjoying this.

Female Speaker: Well, thank you. I'm glad you chose me, then. I want to say, I loved Tamara Hayle. I really love her. She's a great character, and I don't know if you remember me or not. I write books; that's what I do for a living. After I read Tamara Hayle, I said, "I've got to write a mystery." So I would love to know if you could share, what are the most important lessons that you've learned from writing a mystery?

Valerie Wilson Wesley: For mysteries, it's a different kind of writing. It's a genre. You want a strong opening. This is very concrete stuff. You want a good opening, you want to know your character well and make sure you have the clues. You have to introduce the killer within I would say, first three chapters. You never want to bring somebody at the end who has done all this awful stuff, because it doesn't make sense to the reader. It has to be subtle—it's like playing chess in a way. You know who the killer is, but the reader doesn't know. So it's kind of a game you play with him or her, it's teasing and not teasing. Did he build somebody up only to knock him off? So you throw things back. They're fun to write. They're hard to write. People often dismiss these kinds of books. My books are also in Germany, France and in Poland. I've noticed, when I go to Germany to do book tours, they call them crime novels. It's a different kind of approach to them.

Those are the main things that you want to remember. Again, it goes back to character. Make your characters as strong as you can. I outline my mysteries, so I know from chapter to chapter what the peak is going to be, how it's going to flow, what the rhythm of the novel is, because pacing is essential in a good mystery. It must be paced well. So this happens, this happens, this happens, and finally the denouement, everything is revealed. I hope that's helpful.

Female Speaker: It is. Thank you so much.

Valerie Wilson Wesley: You're welcome. I think we're getting the sign to wrap it up from this lovely lady. [Applause] Thank you, sweetheart.

Richard Wesley: Well, thank you, Valerie and thank you for a very delightful evening.

CHAPTER NINE

Art and Politics in Publishing

Moderator: Linda Duggins
Panelists: Tonya M. Evans, Malaika Adero, and Manie Barron

This is a nuts and bolts panel that every aspiring writer will greatly relish. The panelists are all veteran publishing industry insiders. The picture they paint is often not very pretty, but they cover all the bases and will give the writer maybe not what they want to hear, but what they need to hear.

Linda Duggins: In the African-American section of the bookstore someone noted that the book covers looked more like pornography, and questioned what could be between those pages. Was it literature or what? Clearly, the proliferation of these titles is taking place across the country in black bookstores, mainstream bookstores and every vendor table that we pass. The titles seem to be geared towards a younger audience, influenced more by TV, music videos and hip-hop culture, but apparently there are other Black readers of all ages scooping those books up.

Larry Neal talked about art in revolution. He was talking about a Black art that sticks to the ribs, and art that through the strength of its ingredients, the form, the content, the craft, the technique illuminates something special about the living culture of the nation, and by extension, reveals something fundamental about man on this planet. He said the poet; the writer is a key bearer of culture. Nick Chiles posed a few questions related to these issues in a *New York Times* op ed essay, "Their Eyes Were Reading Smut" (January 4, 2006) and this afternoon I'd like to talk about that with the panelists and with you, because we really do have a lot to talk about.

Where are the writers and the publishers in the Black community going from here? Is there a way to go? Are we in deep, deep trouble? Or can we really see our way through this thing? I'd like for Tonya, Malaika and Manie to share a little bit about themselves and their views on this, just for maybe about five minutes or so. Then we're going to open up for discussion with all of us.

Tonya M. Evans: I think this issue has been very well framed for us today, and I hope that we will have a very interesting and engaging discussion, because this affects us all from many different angles. The great majority of us in this room are writers; some are also publishers, and all of us are hopefully readers, and hopefully avid readers. We really need to analyze where we are. Take a step back and look at the history of how "Black literature" and work written by and for an African or African-American audience has developed. Where do we stand now and where do we as a people, even a very diverse people, want to see it go?

There are many good things about Black publishing. I formed a publishing company in 1999. I'm known as a lawyer by day, and a poet by night. I always knew that it was a great challenge to get a major publisher to publish me because I wasn't Nikki Giovanni. I wasn't Sonia Sanchez. It was not going to sell itself off of a shelf. People would have to hear me perform to do it, so back of the room sales would be great, but this may not be a traditional path for me.

The formation of my publishing company was very successful for me. The first book continues to sell, and I did a reprinting. I usually do about 2,000. That was at a time when I was doing a lot of traveling too, and it served me well. It was a way to connect with people and have them take a piece of "my stuff" away with them.

With the second title, I took off my creative hat and focused on the business side of how to connect with people in the way of packaging. Packaging a CD on the inside back cover of my books was also a great way to get out there. The name of the company is FYOS Entertainment (Find Your Own Shine). I was also interested not just in my own work, but also promoting the work of other self-published authors, because I believe there is strength in numbers. Part of my frustration with where we are as a literary people is there is too much division and separation and "what's in it for me," and not "what does my work in isolation, when it is joined with the work of others, do for the black literary experience."

One of the things that I always say is, at least people are reading. I liken it to an experience of how your palette may appreciate white Zinfandel one year, and may appreciate Muscatel as you mature in your wine drinking experience, if that's something that you do. Maybe that might be the pathway that some people will take in order to get over the hump of not reading at all. When you think of reading as entertainment, then you are really competing with music videos, TV, and the two hour quick fix of a movie. You actually have to take time to read a book. It's all about time. We're living in a society that moves very quickly.

I'm coming from that angle, the independent publisher angle. I welcome many different voices. I think you get into a problem in publishing when there's only one voice or only one representation, or when it's done for money as opposed to for love of the written or spoken word.

Malaika Adero: I'm the Acquisitions Editor for Atria, Simon and Schuster. I've been involved in acquisitions and editing since the mid-1980s. Long before that I was an avid reader, worked on a literary journal in high school and so on. My personal background and personal relationship to books is reflected in how I have performed as a professional. I have very diverse interests. My list at Atria, Simon and Schuster, ranges on the fiction side, from literary authors such as Maryse Conde, Tananarive Due, Jewell Parker Rhodes, and Walter Mosley, to urban and hip-hop lit authors such as Shannon Holmes and Daniel Santiago. Each are best selling authors in their own right.

It is actually easier on the fiction side for me to say what I don't like categorically, not even what I don't like, because it's not a matter of what we like or dislike all the time when you're working in this business, but a matter of being able to identify an audience for particular kind of work of a particular writer. You have some affinity for it, because as an editor, as a publisher, just like as a writer, if you don't have an affinity for the subject, for the voice, you should probably leave it alone, no matter how wonderful it is.

I say what's good for the gander in this business is not what's good for the goose. I say this to explain my perspective and my position on this issue of "Their Eyes Were Reading Smut," because I have my intellectual higher artistic side, and then I have the side of me that likes a little smut. [Laughter] It's quite healthy.

What I don't get so much are the in-the-middle-kind of chick lit, or suburban relationship and romance stories, but that's just me. That's one of the things as a writer, (those of you in the audience who are published or looking to be published), that you have to consider in your journey to be published. To have a career as an author means that what is good for the gander, publishing wise, is not good for the goose. You may be brilliant. You may have a book that will be a best seller. You may be the best thing since sliced bread, and you may not be somebody that anyone at this table should necessarily work with for that reason alone.

My position, vis-à-vis, the editorial that Nick Chiles did, is that I share his lament that our standards in this country, not just those of Black people, not just those of French people, not just any kind of people, are very low as far as culture is concerned. I want for us to appreciate more excellence in visual art, excellence in music, and excellence in literature. The hardest part of my job is selling a good book. Let me change that. The hardest part of my job is selling a great book. We can publish good books all day long, engaging stories, but the higher on the cultural food chain, as it were, the more difficult it is to sell. Those things, which are literary, you all might aspire to that, and it's a worthy aspiration, but that often does not come with any kind of material or commercial success.

On the other end of the scale, you can sometimes throw words on a page, as Linda said, and make a little money, but there is always more than that. We'll get to talking about that too. There is art in smut. The other thing that you need to know is that some people complain about the excellence and the lowering of our standards, but the same writers that come to me are often the same writers who will say to me as an editor, "Okay, what can I write that's going to make me some money?"

So you have to reconcile that within yourself as a writer, as a publisher, and as a reader. I don't want to go on and on talking about this because I don't really know what you're interested in as far as what I do, and far as what other particular positions I have on this. So I'll wait for the conversation, the questions, and throw it to my colleague. We struggle back and forth, because he's the one who sells me on your work. [Laughter] He's the first line of defense. In general, people like me don't want to talk to you unless you've gone through people like him.

Manie Barron: When I was an editor, when I was a person like her, I thought that people like me were the spawn of the devil. [Laughter] When I became an agent, I had agents call me up and said, "How dare you. You talked about us like a dog, and now you became one." Once I came on this side, I saw that we were doing God's work. [Laughter] So this conversation that we're going through now, that Nick wrote about, isn't new. We've been having this conversation forever. It's been going on in cycles just like so much of Black art is cyclical, because life is cyclical. I want to read you a passage from something that James Weldon Johnson wrote in 1929 that was published in *Crisis* magazine, and the article is called "Negro Authors and White Publishers":

> There is one complaint that some younger Negro writers are uttering with greater and greater insistence, which I do not
>
> think is based in the facts and which reacts to the injury of the writers uttering it. This complaint is that the leading white publishers have set a standard that Negro writers must conform to or go unpublished. That this standard calls only for books depicting the Negro in a manner which tends to degrade him in the eyes of the world. That only books about the so-called lower types of Negroes and lower faces of Negro life finds consideration and acceptance. Now, in the first place there is a certain snobbishness in terming the less literate and less sophisticated, the more simple and more primitive classes of Negro as lower. At least as literary material, they are higher. They have greater dramatic and artistic potentialities for the writer than the so-called higher classes who so closely resemble the white classes. The vicious and criminal elements, and we must admit that even in our own race, there are such elements, are rightly termed lower, but even they have more

accessible dramatic values then the ordinary, respectable middle class element. It takes nothing less than supreme genius to make middle class society, black or white, interested, to say nothing of making it dramatic.

[Laughter] That was 1929. So here we are, gathered here today, on a Sunday having this same talk. When I was a kid, my father gave me a paint-by-numbers *Last Supper*, which I did. It kept me out of trouble sometimes. Now when I finished it, I didn't go out, get a frame, put it on the wall, and think of it as a piece of art. No, that was a creative endeavor that I did. The real thing by DaVinci—that's a piece of art. We sometimes have not learned to separate creative endeavor from art.

Everything does not have to be art. There is no way on God's earth you're going to tell me Danielle Steel is art, but she is one of the biggest selling mainstream writers, where there are no discussions going on somewhere far in the land among white people saying, "You know, Danielle Steel, art, what's the deal? You know what happened?" That doesn't go on, but for us, we get so caught up into this because of the oppression, because of what we've gone through that I think sometimes we feel everything must be viewed with a lot more weight than it all has to be.

There is a time for junk food. There is a time, yes, I love a good steak, but every now and then, I get this hankering to go to Tad's. I just have a taste for that. So I think what we need to do is have a discussion of how do we meld together, and accept the creative endeavors and the art, and understand that the two can co-exist. Neither one should feel any shame about co-habituating that space, which is a shelf in the library; because they are both doing the same desired end result. Getting somebody to read.

Malaika Adero: In terms of that Manie, the writing aspect of it, the craft of it, the stringing a sentence together properly, I hear what you're saying about the junk food. Every now and again, I like junk food, but I like different kinds of junk food, so how do we attempt to even start that with these publishers. They're basically deciding who gets to eat what junk food.

Manie Barron: I think there is a false assumption, or somewhat false, in that the mainstream publishers are taking the worst of our society and trying to force feed it down our throats, because they're not. By large, you have to remember the publishing industry is made up of well-meaning liberals. People that have fought for and continue to fight for ideas of freedom, the freedom of ideas and being able to have conversations, controversy and debate. So in many ways they're the ones that have been on the line in the publishing industry of trying to bring black voices to the public before the rest of the white world wanted to hear it.

In many ways, and me as someone who talks to them and talks to so many editors, the majority who are white are not feeling this street lit either. They also feel that it is a blight on society, because they have always wanted the best for us, because they have always been fighting for the oppressed, whoever the oppressed may be.

Female Speaker: But they're white.

Manie Barron: Yes, they are, but this still bothers them also. So you don't see it as much as you would think. I hear editors now going, "Oh well, we have one." Meaning a street lit author. So not that they are looking for more, they are like, "No, we have one." Or it has not worked like we've read on the streets, so we're backing away. I disagree that there is this overriding force going on that supports the idea that publishers are only trying to only look for street lit writers.

Tonya M. Evans: I disagree as well, because I think Manie is right. I don't know how well meaning they are, but many publishers and editors in the industry, in terms of self-interest and forgetting altruism and social responsibility, are book nerds. In our

170

aspirations, what we really want to do is to discover a Pulitzer Prize winner or a Nobel Prize winner, so we'll have those brownie points. We're not trying to win brownie points for the average intellectual or pseudo or whatever.

Maliaka Adero: That's true, the social responsibility gets to be a more individual thing, but aside from that, as a business, we have to balance. Every editor I know in order to keep his or her job, has to balance the titles that they acquire: the ones that give them self fulfillment, with the ones that keep them in a job and keep the balance sheet in the black. You do that however you can. Some of us do it by acquiring in addition to literary fiction, narrative non-fiction puzzle books. One of my colleagues is keeping his job because he is acquiring sudoku, which everybody is crazy about now.

My balance sheet looks good because on one end I have erotic literature, which is widely successful, mainly Zane, thank God, [laughter] so that I can publish the Carl Hancock Rux, and the Maryse Conde. I'm a little annoyed with this dumping on urban lit, hip-hop lit and equating that with incompetence or lack of education, because across the board, most of the manuscripts that I read, that are sent to me, hard work has gone into them. Some of them are bad and not well executed, but it's not a blight on anybody's character. My writing is bad most of the time too, until I work on it and work on it, and work on it. If I'm lucky enough to have the right mentors or the right people to read and give me feedback, it comes out all right.

It was so interesting, Saturday I came home. I had been out of town for a week and had gotten a letter, an editorial letter, in response to a piece that I submitted to an anthology that I was commissioned to do a few years ago. It's a long story so I had really forgotten about the piece, and I hadn't looked at it in a few years. This was one of the harshest editorial critiques I had ever seen, and they were saying that about me, [laughter] and that's my job. I was saying, "Okay, I would have put it differently." I would have been a little more gentle about my author's feelings, but okay, I'm a big girl. I can take it and I'll rewrite the piece.

Tonya M. Evans: When you have booksellers saying urban lit—this bookseller from Walden Books said, "Hip-hop fiction is doing for the 15 to 25 year old, African-American, what Harry Potter did for kids." That to me is like a mouthful.

Malaika Adero: It is a mouthful, but this says more about him then it does about the literature. I'll tell you why. I think that hip-hop and urban lit is a good thing for young people. I think that when they are badly published and badly edited it is a bad thing. Now a lot of that is because these are young people doing this by the seat of their pants. They have the industry and the self-determination, and I understand because I'm a poet too, and I self-published in the late 1970s. I made some lunch money.

They have a business savvy that we can learn from with our artistic aspirations. We have a knowledge and experience that they can learn from. What we need to not do is keep talking about the other as the enemy, and talk about how we can dialogue and share our knowledge and experience to work together. My solution for moving beyond this conversation that we keep having decade after decade is to move more into ownership.

We have to have some self-determination. When you go to somebody else's house for dinner, you can't go to their house and tell them what to cook and how to cook. You need to just go home and have your own dinner party, and that's what I'm going to do. I don't get it confused. I work for Atria, Simon and Schuster, and my goals, visions, and aspirations for what I want for myself professionally overlap with that corporation, but do not begin and end with that corporation. There are things that I want to do as a publisher, as an artist, as a writer that are not going to get done in the context of my job at Atria, Simon and Schuster. I don't expect it to.

You have to be honest. You have to know what your

position is, what role you're going to play, and play that, and be clear about that. If there is something else that you want, like ownership, like more control, like a policy making decision, then you have to create your own thing.

Female Speaker: Tonya, what are some of the things you recommend for the authors that you work with?

Tonya M. Evans: We have such a great opportunity now because of where we are in the industry. Access and whether we're going to have self-determination are very powerful ideas for me and my firm of which I'm now sole practitioner. I've started at large firms, major firms and did all the right things, and have an impressive resume, but I knew that I was bigger than that, that I couldn't work there seven days a week for somebody else, making money that was nice, six figure money. It's nothing like I make now. I work for myself and actually have a better quality of life for my family, so I wanted to piggyback off of that too, just for a moment.

Something that we can do is to remember that every person who writes is not going to be a good business person. You may not want to be in the confines of somebody else telling you what to do or say, but you may not wear a business hat very well. You might be completely and totally creative, so you really have to look and first decide am I the type of person who can really take off my creative hat. Then look at the book, not as your baby, which as I look at all my books as babies until I put on my publishing hat and say, "How can I move this unit?" It may sound harsh, but it really is a way to become savvy about the business. When you think of the Zane's and the Relentless Aaron's of the world who are quite business savvy about finding out what people want and how to get it to them.

I work with many people to review and negotiate contracts. Agents are the place to go if you want placement, but oftentimes people come to me to say, "This is what the agent said. Now you tell me, does it say that?"

Actually, I have a symbiotic relationship with agents so it can work very well, but you really have to be business savvy about how you approach this. I think if you're going to do that, then also understand the awesome responsibility. With great power comes great responsibility. You have all of this. You have your own publishing company. What are you going to put out? Is it going to be indistinguishable from the Simon and Schuster books of the world, or is it going to look mom and pop. So you want to bring the excellence that we speak about, regardless of what your genre is, to make sure that you are taken seriously, and that you don't have 2,000 books in your driveway and are unable to move them to the 2,000 people that would love to read them.

Female Speaker: That responsibility you talked about is on the business side, but how do we fit in the responsibility to the Black community? Do writers think about that? All three of you, I know we think about it, but as you go through your day-to-day, where is the responsibility? Baldwin says we should write, but we should tell the truth. But whose truth are we talking about? Our truth or their truth?

Tonya M. Evans: As a personal thing, from a spiritual and religious perspective, I want to focus on a certain type of business and the way I want to define myself. So it becomes how do you want to be represented in the world? What do you want to leave after you have passed on? What legacy are you leaving? What footprint are you leaving? How do you want people to remember you? I always believe that in the creative process, you have to just focus and get it out of you, but then you have to go back to your editing, positioning and all those other things.

We all know people who brag about how quickly they can write a book and how many books in a short period of time. That's not necessarily a great way to go. If you love the written and spoken word, and you want to memorialize your place in this world by what you leave from a literary perspective, then it's a greater responsibility than just trying to make money. I always shy away from people who say that, and there are a lot of people who come and do say, "What do I need to do to make some money." I practice law to make money. Oddly enough, some of the books have started to sell, but that wasn't my purpose. I wanted a way to connect to people and then I believe I was blessed in a certain way to continue to do that, but if I never made another penny off a poetry book, or even the legal reference guides, I'd still do it, because it's not about the money. You can always learn how to put sentences together if you are so inclined; it's the money chasing in this culture that concerns me.

Malaika Adero: The late Octavia Butler said something that stuck in my mind. She said that everything that you write about, you advertise. You have to think about that—everything that you write about. I know that from being an author myself. Don't write about any subject that you don't want to talk about for the rest of your life. It's an easy thing to say, but luckily for me, the first full-length book that I published was on the African-American migration, the migratory phenomenon. I can talk about that for the rest of my life because it is interesting enough and I'm passionate enough about it.

My most recent book was on Zora Neale Hurston, and I can talk about that. Just as you may have to live with the reputation you leave on prom night, so the writer has to live with the reputation of what he has written.

Tonya is right. You have to decide that for yourself. That's not something that can be legislated in this room or by anybody else, but we all can contribute.

The other solution is that we all do our part in promoting excellence, which means people have to see you reading the good things. They have to hear you listening to the good things and watching the good things. We steal from each other; we borrow from each other. Everybody wants the good thing that somebody else has, so let somebody else see you demonstrating your values. If that is what you value—books are also like movies. The best books are the ones that tend to make the least money.

Learn how to promote yourself, to get noticed. What my boss dictates to me is: "Why aren't you on that?" They're not sitting around thinking, "Okay, how can we just damage further the mental health of Black people." They're not thinking about us at all, but they are saying, "I see this guy everywhere." They knock on my door and they say, "Malaika, what's with this guy? Can we get him? Can we do it for him?" Whatever you want to see, you talk about, you promote and we'll surely follow.

Manie Barron: I was once a buyer for Golden Leaves Book Distributors, a national wholesaler. Golden Leaves was selling to bookstores all over. This was really early in the black book experience that we know now. In addition, when Terry McMillan's *Disappearing Acts* came out, I managed a bookstore. I had to hand sell it by saying it had been optioned by Denzel Washington, because women didn't know who Terry McMillan was. So I've watched this explosion and I've been in there while it was going on.

When I was a buyer for black interest titles, I would see a Simon and Schuster rep once a year, and that was when they were selling the winter list. They would have their one black book a year.

When I would see the rep come in, and I'd go, "Gary, you have nothing for me, it's not February, right?"

"Yes," and he'd keep right on going. Now Simon and Schuster has become one of the main publishers that has been publishing African American lit. There wasn't any big sea change that went on in terms of their feelings. They didn't become more embracing of African American culture and people. It was money. Yes, it was about money. Everything is about the money, and as Malaika has said they are looking at what you purchase. That is the determining factor of everything else that's done.

There was that piece that ran on Relentless Aaron; publishers who had never done street lit were calling me the next day going, "What have you got?" Why, because Relentless Aaron was on the front page of the arts section of the *New York Times*, the paper of record. This is what it's all about. Unless you're controlling it, you're in the hands of those that do. In their own way, they think that they're giving you what you want, because they're looking at what you spend. They're not really trying to dictate; they're trying to follow. They're trying to get more out of you by what they think you're looking for, so if you don't want those books, then you have to buy the other one. You have to send the message to them about what it is you're looking for because that's what they want. They want what you're looking for, because that way, they get your money.

Malaika Adero: Speaking of buyers, because they are my favorite people to pick on actually, and the biggest encumbrance between readers and me. We can publish a range of great literature from good to bad to indifferent, but if we have to get the orders, we have to get the support of the retailers who sell books. They are becoming more and more varied. It used to be bookstores. Now we're talking about trying to schmooze and court Target, Wal-Mart and whoever else all over the country. Sam's Club, BJ's, so there have been other sea changes going on in the industry that I and other editors are trying to catch up to. I've never before until this year, been sent out by my company to go out and talk to buyers like that, but we're doing that now so that we can come to terms, and so that the book buyers and sellers can identify more with publishing people.

Female Speaker: Malaika, are we also saying to you, "You go out and sell those books because we don't know how to?"

Malaika Adero: Yes.

Female Speaker: So when the publisher says to the white sales force, "Okay, here are our fall selections," and they go, "Damn, how are we going to convince the sales force to go out there and push this particular book?" its because they need a little more support from people like you who understand what the writing is and what the story is.

Malaika Adero: No, you're right. Most sales forces are white, and if you have any young people in your life and they need to consider career options, please, talk to them about publishing and sales because we need people on the sales and marketing side. It's very frustrating for me to publish good books and then have people who can't translate them. I look at field reports from sales reps all the time, and sometimes I'm just pulling my hair out because we're writing them memos, writing them briefs, and giving them Cliff Notes, because of course, they don't have time to read every book. Then I did hear a rep say, "Well, I didn't push this in my territory because in this territory they don't like Jamaican novels, when Maryse Conde is from Guadalupe."

The novel is set in Tokyo and South Africa and New York. Really, that's true, but the other point to sending editors out there in the field though, is for the people on that end of the sales end to identify with editors period, black, white or indifferent and our language in our process. So it's both recruiting more Blacks in sales and marketing and helping people in sales and marketing identify with editors and learn how to translate books.

Manie Barron: From my perspective there is one thing that everybody knows about Black folks, that we love church. We go to church. That's the one thing that white people know. The world knows, so I have a photographic book that was going to be the first book on the Black church. There have been *Crowns*, but that was really about the hats and there have been books about individual churches, but this is a book celebrating the Black America, the Black worship experience in America. I sent it to publishers all over, and it's a gorgeous book. It had a foreword by Gordon Park; it has beautiful photography.

This man went out and decided he would shoot churches

178

based on the size of the media market of African-Americans. So this man plotted this also. It was marketing and editorial brilliance. I went out with this proposal, went to everybody. I wound up having an auction with just two publishers, and I had Thomas Nelson, the biggest Bible publisher in the world; now if anybody gets God, it's them. [Laughter] They told me that they didn't know how to sell this.

Female Speaker: It's not the same God though, Manie.

Manie Barron: Right. Evidently. [Laughter] It's a different God, and they rejected this book because they didn't know what to do. I had other publishers tell me "We don't know how to sell it." This is what I know; you don't need to sell it. Print it. We will come to it. If you print it, we will come, because this is one of those that will sell itself. But publishers, even with all that has gone, what they have watched in the past 10 or so years in the proliferation of black book buying, they still don't get it. They still don't get us. They still keep a distance. So with all of those numbers, you would think that there would be a little bit more of proximity, but there isn't. They still have the walls there, so in many ways you are having the same fight over and over and over again. Imagine every morning when you drive to work and you had to put your car together again, every morning before you get into it and drive it, so this is what that process is like.

All of this comes into it, whether the art versus, shall we call it, not art. Should we uplift the race, or should we let the good times roll. All of this is part and parcel of this whole experience.

Malaika Adero: Manie's book is a good example because I passed on that book as well. The reason I passed on that book is that we Atria, Simon and Schuster, the company I work with are not quite equipped yet to work the church community.

Manie Barron: The nontraditional books.

Malaika Adero: What I mean by that and this is a good example because it also speaks to what the author can bring to the situation, too. The A.M.E church has tens of thousands of members. And those of you who go to conventions every year know that there are thousands of people coming to the convention, with pockets full of money to spend on the convention floor. We're not set up to sell at those kind of conventions, so that's for naught. We don't know that. We're not familiar with the kind of organizations to speak with whoever their communications people are, and their marketing people in order to promote, to stage an event such as the National Baptist Convention, which also, pockets money. That's where our people are. If the company, the professionals, doesn't have the mechanism for communicating with them, if you don't have a dialogue and relationship with those kind or organizations, then they don't know what to do.

Female Speaker: That always blows my mind because that's a phone call. I happen to know this particular author, and he had, I kid you not, he had a marketing proposal like this that he worked on for 10 years. When I looked at it, I said, "Wow, he could team up with a publicist and they could rock the country." But the publicists are not forward thinking enough to do that.

Malaika Adero: That's where the beauty of the independent publishing world comes in. More than a few of my clients started off self-publishing, and eventually were picked up. This happens when you have great flexibility in the nontraditional sales market. If it's going to be back of the room sales, or if it's going to be the church circuit, If you already have a built-in audience and you know how to access it, then there is the opportunity to go forward on an independent basis, whether or not that's ultimately your goal to do it forever. It's a lot of work. It's all day, everyday. It's no joke, but if you're an author signed to a major house, you have to do your work too. I tell them to take that little advance that you have and go get a fabulous publicist, have them work together with

180

the in-house publicist.

If you're positioned in a way that nontraditional sales may be your avenue, then the independent route, at least initially, may be your best route.

Manie Barron: This isn't a shortness of vision that only goes on when they look at black books. They are just as myopic with their own books. [Laughter] It's not like we should be asking them to do more for us than they do for themselves. So that's another thing that you also have to keep in mind. This is just the industry that doesn't do what it should do as a mass media to reach out to the people. When you look at the number for opening weekend for even a bad movie, a movie that they said has flopped, there are more eyes that have seen that movie, then have seen one of our top selling books, and I'm just talking about publishing, not black, not white, just publishing. There are more eyes that have seen that bad movie then have seen a book, even one of the "best books," by whoever's definition. It's an economy of scale, so we have to also take that into consideration.

Female Speaker: Hi, I'm Shaunda Buchanan. Malaika, who are your nonfictional authors?

Malaika Adero: Ellis Cose is one. Dr. Price Cobbs, *My American Journey from Rage* is another title. Kevin Mile, *Make It Happen: The Hip-hop Generation Guide to Success*. I publish a lot of memoirs including the memoir of Gordon Parks, and Dr. Price Cobbs, who has a memoir, and Stephanie Stokes Oliver, from *Essence*. It's a long, long, long list.

Male Speaker: Two comments, first on ownership. It should be noted that today *The Covenant* published by *Third World Press* is number four on the *New York Times* bestseller list. Second, I think there are some things to learn about the church market, not that any of my work would approach that, but to look at Vy Higgins' success in developing one of the few sustaining black theatre audiences in the City of New York. I think that the approach is obviously not an overlap, but I think there are some parallels in looking at the lessons that she has to teach about that.

Malaika Adero: I think that you're right that it's not just a church market, but the other thing, the third thing that I advocate is looking at new models for marketing and promotion. We need to borrow from the music industry in how you promote the books.

Male Speaker: You have proved a point that I've long suspected as a poet. Indeed, agents do God's work, because every time I think about an agent for poetry, I'm reminded of the eye of the needle.

I know it may be a side issue, I would hope that you all might talk a little bit about self-publishing, which is the direction that many of us are in, not because we want to be, but because we're forced to be, and our work suffers because we are not read. The first time I self-published, I gave away more than I sold. I still have not had a commercial success.

Tonya M. Evans: We also need to learn how to delegate as Black people and work in teams. Even if you have that knowledge, you cannot physically do it all, and do it all at the same time.

Malaika Adero: And do it well.

Tonya M. Evans: Yes, so we have to team up with other people. I'm looking for—if anybody in this audience is a CPA Accountant, talk to me at the end of it, because that's what I'm missing from my team for what I'm trying to do right now.

Manie Barron: You do have to meld and crossover and look at and use other forms to try to reach people, because publishing never does that. Since publishing is built on arrogance in the first place, whenever you try to tell them something they don't know, they don't want to hear it, because they know.

Malaika Adero: Some of us.

Manie Barron: Yes, so it's easy, and I've watched it time and time again. I just shrug my shoulders. At one time I use to get angry, then I just realized that's not going to do anything, so you just find other ways around it. That's to say, "okay, let me go do what has to be done on my own, and my folks, we go do that." My clients, we find other ways to get the end result. Once you realize that that impudence is there, instead of just standing there with your nose pressed to the wall, banging on it saying, "Come on guys, open it for me." You just walk around yourself.

Malaika Adero: The thing is, and one of the reasons for that is it's not for lack of, if you talk to individual people in publishing many of them would agree with your sentiment, but what can be done by a smaller, more independent company that can move more quickly is different from what can be done by a big corporation. These bureaucracy-laden institutions do not move quickly, so that's why I aspire to be an independent publisher, because I can do some creative things in an easier way than I can in a company where we're publishing 500 books a year, or a thousand books a year. You have to, to some degree, do things in a cookie cutter fashion in the same mold, because that structure also doesn't allow for you to have the head count ever. There you need to do all this stuff. Publishing is time consuming.

Male Speaker: As a self-published author, I'm learning some hard lessons that I'm trying to address right now, and I'm sure other self-published authors probably face the same dilemma. I publish and I have a bigger project that I could have done first. As an unknown author I chose to publish the book first, and tried to attract the attention of publishers. It just didn't generate. So my question to you is what are some of the methods that you recommend that self-

183

published authors use to really attract the attention of the mainstream publishers to a project?

Manie Barron: It all comes down to the units. Once somebody has sold some books, that's when a publisher will take interest. Now, there is also a chalk line here too, which is: what the saturation level for a book is? When is the tipping point? When has it sold enough on the street level that it has reached where it is level, it's watermarked. A publisher may not be able to move it anymore than that, so a publisher will look at the numbers. Yes, they want you to have a lot of sales, but you can't have so many, that they think that there will not still be more people to get. It's a hard balance, but the best thing is when a book is just really starting to be at an accelerated pace. The normal curve is very slow. When you are a self-published author, your media is your friends and your family, in most cases. Yes, there is the Internet, but you are usually using word of mouth, so it's a longer lag time, rhetorical before it gets out into the ether. By the time it starts to accelerate, and you are selling some books, and starting to rise, that's when publishers are interested.

Tonya M. Evans: That's when you first acquire that self-published title, it'll disappear for awhile. They'll want to catch it on the upswing, and they want it to disappear, so people are talking among themselves and they're generating interest and they can't get it, so when it hits again, then there is this resurgence of interest.

Malaika Adero: Yes, and you have to get as much media as you can, because what happens sometimes is you saturate your regional market, but you have no national market. In order to have a national audience, the word has to get out on a national level. That's when you need to partner with somebody. Try to get reviewed. I just saw a self-published author on the *Today Show* the other day, and I was like, "Whoa." That's major. Let me see if I can figure out how to call them up, and I'm sure that 20 of my colleagues would try and call them up that morning too.

BIBLIOGRAPHY

Adero, Malaika. and Lucy Hurston. *Speak, So You Can Speak Again: The Life of Zora Neale Hurston.* New York: Doubleday, 2004.

Adero, Malaika. *Up South: Stories, Studies and Letters of This Century's African\American Migrations.* New York: The New Press, 1992.

Ali, Mohammed N. *The Prophet of Zongo Street : Stories.* New York: Amistad, 2005.

Barnes, Steven. *Great Sky Woman: A Novel.* New York: One World/Ballantine, 2006.
———. *Lion's Blood: A Novel of Slavery and Freedom in Alternate America.* New York: Warner Books, 2003.
———. *Charisma.* New York: Forge, 2003.
———. *Zulu Heart.* New York: Tor Books, 2001.
———. *Iron Shadows.* New York: Tor Books, 2000.

Beauford, Fred. *The King of Macy's.* Irvington: Morton Books, 2006.
———. *The Year Jerry Garcia Died.* Irvington: Morton Books, 2001.
———. *The Hard Luck Novel.* Irvington: Morton Books, 2001.
———. *The Womanizer.* Irvington: Morton Books, 2000.
———. *The Rejected American.* Irvington: Morton Books, 2000.
———. *Conversations with Albert Murray* (Literature Conversation Series), Jackson: University Press of Mississippi, 1997.
———. *Conversations with Ernest Gaines* (Literature

Conversation Series), Jackson: University Press of Mississippi 1995.

Boyd, Herb and Yusef Lateef. *The Gentle Giant*. Irvington: Morton Books, 2006.

Boyd, Herb. *Heroes of America: Martin Luther King, Jr*. Edina: Abdo, 2005.
———. *The Harlem Reader: A Celebration Pound for Pound: A Biography of Sugar Ray Robinson of New York's Most Famous Neighborhood*, from the *Renaissance Years to the 21st Century*. New York: Three Rivers Press, 2003.
———. *We Shall Overcome: The History of the Civil Rights Movement As It Happened* (Book with 2 Audio CDs). Naperville: Sourcebooks Mediafusion; Book & CDEd., 2004.
———. *Race and Resistance: African-Americans in the Twenty-First Century*. MA: South End Press, 2002.
———. *Down the Glory Road: Contributions of African Americans in United States History and Culture*. New York: Avon 1995.

Boyd, Valerie. *Wrapped In Rainbows: The Life of Zora Neale Hurston*. New York: Lisa Drew, 2004.

Delany, Samuel. *Stars*. CT: Wesleyan University Press, 2005.
———. *About Writing: Seven Essays, Four Letters, and Five Interviews*. CT: Wesleyan University Press, 2005.
———. *The Fall of the Towers*. New York: Vintage, 2004.
———. *The Fall of the Towers: Out of the Dead City, the Towers of Toran*. New York: Vintage, 2004.

———. *Phallos.* MI: Bamberger Books, 2004.

———. *Hogg: A Novel.* Normal: FC2, 2004.

———. *Village.* MI: University of Minnesota Press, 2004.

———. *The Motion of Light in Water: Sex and Science Fiction Writing in the East Village.* MI: University of Minnesota Press, 2004.

———. *Babel-17/Empire Star.* New York: Vintage, 2003.

———. *Aye, and Gomorrah: And Other Stories.* New York: Vintage, 2003.

———. *Nova.* New York:Vintage, 2002.

———. *Dahlgren.* New York: Vintage, 2001.

———. *1984.* Rutherford: Voyant Publishing, 2000.

———. *The Jewels of Aptor.* New York:Gollancz, 2000.

———. *Shorter Views: Queer Thoughts & the Politics of the Para literary.* CT: Wesleyan University Press, 2000.

———. *The Einstein Intersection.* CT: Wesleyan University Press, 1998.

———. *Times Square Red, Times Square Blue.*New York: New York University Press 1999.

———. *Bread & Wine: An Erotic Tale of New York.* New York: Juno, 1999.

———. *Trouble on Triton: An Ambiguous Heterotopia.* CT: Wesleyan University Press, 1996.

———. *They Fly At Ciron.* New York: Tor Fantasy, 1996.

———. *Longer Views: Extended Essays.* CT: Wesleyan University Press, 1996.

———. *The Complete Nebula Award-Winning Fiction of Samuel R. Delany.* New York: Bantam Books, 1986.

Due, Tananarive. *Joplin's Ghost: A Novel.* New York: Atria Publishing, 2005.

———. *The Living Blood.* New York: Washington Square Press, 2002.

———. *The Good House: A Novel.* New York: Atira, 2005.

———. *The Black Rose.* New York: One

World/Ballantine, 2001.

————. *My Soul to Keep.* New York: EOS, 1998.

Evans, Tonya M; Susan Borden Evans; and Dan Poynter.
————. *Literary Law Guide for Authors, Copyrights, Trademarks and Contracts in Plain Language.* PA: FYOS Entertainment/Legal Write Publications, 2003.

Evers-Williams, Myrlie and Manning Marable. *The Autobiography of Medgar Evers A Hero's Life and Legacy Revealed Through His Writings, Letters, and Speeches,* New York: Basic Civitas 2006.

Evers-Williams, Myrlie and Melinda Blau. *Watch Me Fly: What I Learned on the Way to Becoming the Woman I Was Meant to Be.* New York: Little Brown & Co. 1999.

Farley, Christopher John. *Before the Legend: The Rise of Bob Marley.* New York: Amistad/Harper Collins, 2006.
————. *Kingston By Starlight.* New York: Three Rivers Press, 2005.
————. *Aaliyah: More Than a Woman.* MI: Tandem Library, 2001.
————. *My Favorite War.* New York: Ecco Press 1998.

Golden, Marita and E. Lynn, Harris. *Gumbo: A Celebration of African American Writers.* New York: Harlem Moon, 2002.

Golden, Marita and Susan Shreve. *Skin Deep: Black Women & White Women Write About Race.* New York: Anchor, 1996.

Golden, Marita. *After: A Novel.* New York: Doubleday 2006.
————. *Don't Play in the Sun: One Woman's Journey Through the Color Complex.* New York: Anchor, 2005.

———. *Migrations of the Heart (An Autobiography)*. New York: Anchor, 2005.

———. *A Miracle Everyday.* New York: Anchor 1999.

———. *The Edge of Heaven*. New York: One World/Ballantine 1999.

———. *And Do Remember Me*. New York: Ballantine 1994.

———. *Saving Our Sons*. New York: Doubleday 1994.

———. *Wild Women Don't Wear No Blues*. New York: Anchor, 1994.

———. *Long Distance Life*. New York: Ballantine, 1992.

Greene, Brenda M. with Elizabeth Nunez. Eds. *Defining Ourselves: Black Writers in the 90s*. New York: Peter Lang, 1999.

Greene, Brenda with Lil Brannon. Eds. *Rethinking American Literature*. Urbana: National Council of Teachers of English, 1996

Jackson, Linda Susan. *What Yellow Sounds Like*. Evanston: Tia Chucha 2007.

Madhubuti, Haki R. *Yellow Black: The First Twenty-One Years of a Poet's Life, A Memoir*. Chicago: Third World Press, 2005.

———. *Rise Vision Comin*. CD. Chicago: Third World Press, 2004.

———. *Run Toward Fear: New Poems and a Poet's Handbook*, Chicago: Third World Press, 2004.

———. *Tough Notes: A Healing Call for Creating Exceptional Black Men*, Chicago: Third World Press, 2002.

———. *HeartLove: Wedding and Love Poems*. Third World Press, 1998.

———. *Groundwork: New and Selected Poems of Don L. Lee/ Haki R. Madhubuti, 1966-1996*. Third World Press,

1996.

———. *Claiming Earth: Race, Rage Rape, Redemption: Blacks Seeking a Culture of Enlightened Empowerment.* Third World Press, 1994.

———. *Black Men, Obsolete, Single, Dangerous.* Chicago: Third World Press, 1990.

McKible, Adam. Introduction to *When Washington Was in Vogue* by Edward Christopher Williams. 2005. New York: Amistad.

———. *The Space and Place of Modernism: The Little Magazine in New York* (Literary Criticism and Cultural Theory). New York: Routledge, 2002.

Mosley Walter. *The Wave.* Lebanon: Aspect, 2006.

———. *Fortunate Son: A Novel.* New York: Little Brown, 2006.

———. *Life Out of Context.* London: Nation, 2006.

———. *Cinnamon Kiss: A Novel.* New York: Little, Brown, 2005.

———. *47.* New York: Little, Brown, 2005.

———. *Little Scarlet: An Easy Rawlins Mystery.* New York: Little, Brown, 2004.

———. *The Man in My Basement: A Novel.* New York: Little, Brown, 2004.

———. *Fear Itself.* Ukiah: Orion 2004.

———. *Bad Boy Brawly Brown.* New York: Warner, 2003.

———. *Six Easy Pieces: Easy Rawlins Stories.* New York: Washington Square Press 2003.

———. *Fear Itself: A Fearless Jones Novel.* New York: Little, Brown, 2003.

———. *What Next: A Memoir Toward World Peace.* Baltimore: Black Classic Press, 2003.

———. *Black Betty: Featuring an Original Easy Rawlins Short Story "Gator Green".* New York: Warner, 2002.

———. *Futureland.* New York: Warner 2002.

———. *Devil in a Blue Dress.* New York: Washington Square

Press, 2002.

———. *White Butterfly: Featuring an Original Easy Rawlins Short Story Lavender.* New York: Washington Square Press, 2002.

———. *A Little Yellow Dog: Featuring an Original Easy Rawlins Short Story Gray-Eyed*

———. *Death.* New York: Washington Square Press, 2002.

———. *Fearless Jones.* New York: Warner Vision, 2002.

———. *Workin' on the Chain Gang: Shaking Off the Dead Hand of History.* New York: Ballantine, 2000.

———. *Walkin' the Dog.* New York: Back Bay Books, 2000.

———. *Mississippi Blues.* Germany: Golmann, 2000.

———. *Socrates in Watts.* Zurich: Unionsverlag, 2000.

———. *Blue Light.* New York: Aspect, 1999.

———. *Always Outnumbered, Always Outgunned.* New York: Washington Square Press, 1998.

———. *Rl's Dream: A Novel.* New York: W.W. Norton & Company, 1995.

———. *Walter Mosley Omnibus: Devil in a Blue Dress/A Red Death/White Butterfly.* London: Pan Macmillan, 1995.

Nunez, Elizabeth and Jennifer Sparrow. *Stories from Blue Latitudes: Caribbean Women Writers at Home and Abroad.* Berkeley: Seal Press, 2005.

Nunez, Elizabeth. *Prospero's Daughter.* New York: Ballantine Books, 2006.

———. *Bruised Hibiscus.* New York: One World/Ballantine, 2003.

———. *Grace.* New York: One World/Ballantine, 2003.

———. *Discretion.* New York: One World/Ballantine, 2003.

———. *Beyond Limbo Silence.* New York: Ballantine, 2003.

Raboteau, Emily. *The Professor's Daughter.* New York: Henry Holt and Co., 2005.

Reed, Ishmael and David Matlin. *Prisons: Embracing New*

America From Vernooykill Creek to Abu Ghraib.
Berkeley: North Atlantic Books, 2005.

Reed, Ishmael. *New and Collected Poems, 1966-2006.* New
York: Carroll & Graf, 2006.
———. *Under the White Sky.* Xlibris, 2005.
———. *Another Day at the Front.* New York: Basic Books, 2004.
———. *Blues City: A Walk In Oakland.* New York: Crown, 2003.
———. *The Last Days of Louisiana Red.* Champaign Urbana:
Dalkey, 2000.
———. *The Reed Reader.* New York: Basic Books, 2000.
———. *Yellow Back Radio Broke-Down.* Champaign-Urbana:
Dalkey, 2000.
———. *The Flight To Canada.* New York: Scribner, 1998.
———. *Reckless Eyeballing.* Champaign-Urbana: Dalkey, 2000.
———. *The Freelance Pallbearers.* Champaign-Urbana: Dalkey,
1999.
———. *The Terrible Twos.* Champaign-Urbana: Dalkey, 1999.
———. *The Terrible Threes.* Champaign-Urbana: Dalkey, 1999.

———. *Dark Eros: Black Erotic Writings.* New York: St.
Martin's Griffin, 1999
———. *Conversations With Ishmael Reed.* Jackson: University
Press of Mississippi, 1996.
———. *Ishmael Reed: An Interview.* Dallas: Contemporary
Research, 1993.
———. *Japanese By Spring.* New York: Penguin, 1996.
———. *Mumbo Jumbo.* New York: Scribner, 1996
———. *Reed And The Ends With Race.* New York: Penguin, 1996.
———. *Airing Dirty Laundry.* New York: Perseus Books, 1995.
———. *Before Columbus Foundation Fiction Anthology:
Selections from the American Book Awards1980-1990.*
New York: Norton and Company, 1992.

Rux, Carl Hancock. *Asphalt: A Novel.* New York: Washington

Square Press, 2005.

———. *Talk.* New York: Theatre Communications Group, 2003.

———. *Pagan Operetta.* Little Rock: Fly By Night Press,1998.

Thomas, Sheree Renee. *Dark Matter: Reading the Bones.* Lebanon: Aspect, 2004.

———. *Dark Matter: A Century of Speculative Fiction from the African Diaspora.* Lebanon: Aspect, 2000.

Wesley, Valerie Wilson. *Willimena Rules 23 Ways to Mess Up Valentine's Day Book#5.* New York: Jump at the Sun, 2005.

———. *Playing My Mother's Blues* William, New York: Morrow, 2005.

———. *Book 3 Middle Grade Series for Black Girls.* New York: Hyperion, 2005.

———. *Book 4 Middle Grade Series for Black Girls.*New York: Hyperion, 2005.

———. *Willimena and Mrs. Sweetly's Guinea Pig.* New York: Hyperion, 2005.

———. *How to Almost Ruin Your Class Play (Willimena Rules!).* Eastsound: Turtleback, 2005.

———. *How to Lose Your Cookie Money (Willimena Rules! 3).* New York: Scholastic, 2005.

———. *Dying in the Dark: A Tamara Hayle Mystery Tamara Hayle Mystery.* Waterville: Thorndike Press, 2005.

———. *Willimena Rules!: How to Fish for Trouble - Book #2.* New York: Jump At The Sun, 2004.

———. *How to Lose Your Class Pet.* Hampton Fields: Sagebrush, 2003.

———. *When Death Comes Stealing (A Tamara Hale Mystery).* New York: Putnam, 1994.

———. *Always True To You.* New York: William Morrow, 2002.

———. *The Devil Riding.* New York: Avon, 2002.

———. *Ain't Nobody's Business If I Do: A Novel.* New York:

Avon, 2002.

———. *Willimena and The Cookie Money*. New York: Jump At The Sun, 2001.

———. *Easier to Kill (Tamara Hayle Mystery)*. New York: Avon, 1999.

———. *Freedom's Gift: Juneteenth Story.* New York: Simon & Schuster, 1997.

———. *No Hiding Place (Tamara Hayle Mystery).* New York: Putnam, 1997.

———. *Where Evil Sleeps*. New York: Putnam, 1996.

———. *Devil's Gonna Get Him.* New York: Putnam, 1995.

———. *Where Do I Go From Here?* New York: Scholastic, 1993.

Yarbrough, Camille. *Iron Pot Cooker*. Vanguard Records, Audio CD, 2000.

———. *The Shimmershine Queens*. Hampton Falls: Sagebrush, 1999.

———.*Cornrows*. New York: Putnam, 1997.

———.*The Little Tree Growin' in the Shadow.* New York: Putnam, 1996.

EDITORS

Brenda M. Greene is Professor of English and Executive Director of The Center for Black Literature at Medgar Evers College of the City University of New York. Professor Greene served as coordinator of the National Black Writers Conferences (NBWCs) at Medgar Evers and was Director of the 2003 and 2006 NBWC (www.mec.cuny.edu/nbwc). Her research interests are in the areas of the literature of women of color, multicultural literature, and English studies, and she has written a number of essays in these fields. Professor Greene is the co-editor of *Defining Ourselves: Black Writers in the Nineties*, by Peter Lang Publishers and *Rethinking American Literature*, published by the National Council of Teachers of English. She is currently working on a professional memoir.

Fred Beauford founded *Black Creation* magazine in 1969 and it became one of the largest magazines dealing with the famous Black Arts Movement of the 70s. In 1974, Beauford founded *Neworld:The Multi-Cultural Magazine of the Arts*, in Los Angeles. The magazine was the first of its kind, welcoming the entire American family in its pages. In addition, Mr. Beauford served for eight years as the Editor of the Crisis Magazine, the official publication of the NAACP. He has taught at The University of Southern California(USC), UC Berkeley, N.Y.U., Cal State Northridge and SUNY/Old Westbury. Beauford is currently the managing Partner of Morton Books, Inc., the Editor-in-Chief/Publisher of the *Neworld Review* and the author of five novels including the critically acclaimed, *The Year Jerry Garcia Died* and *The King of Macy's* and the best selling collection of essays, *The Rejected American*.

CONTRIBUTORS

Malaika Adero is senior editor at Atria Books/Simon & Schuster. She began her career in publishing more than 20 years ago and has worked with numerous authors, as varied as Zane, Maryse Condé, bell hooks, Wanda Sykes, Wendy Williams, Ellis Cose, Carl Hancock Rux, Spike Lee, Tananarive Due and Susan L. Taylor. Adero was Executive Editor of Amistad Press when it was launched as an independent company. She is coauthor with Dr. Lucy Hurston of *Speak, So You Can Speak Again: The Life of Zora Neale Hurston* (Doubleday, 2004) and author/editor of *Up South: Stories, Studies and Letters of This Century's African American Migrations* (The New Press, 1992).

Mohammed Naseehu Ali is a native of Ghana. A writer and musician, Ali's fiction and essays have been published in *The New Yorker*, the *New York Times, Mississippi Review, Gathering of the Tribes* and *Essence*. His collection of short fiction *The Prophet of Zongo Street* (Amistad, 2005) locates him in the tradition of classic African writers such as Amos Tutuola and Chinua Achebe. Ali lives in Brooklyn with his wife and two daughters.

Steven Barnes has published over three million words of fiction, including the Endeavor Award-winning *Lion's Blood* and the New York Times bestseller *Beowulf's Children*. He wrote the Emmy-winning " A Stitch in Time" episode of *The Outer Limits,* and has been nominated for the Hugo, Nebula, and Cable Ace awards. He was the first black author to write novels in either the Star Trek series (*Far Beyond the Stars*) or Star Wars (*The Cestus Deception).*

Manie Barron has been in the world of books for over fifteen years. He spent over seven years at Random House where he worked on marketing and promotion of all of Random House's African American title. Barron also began what is now the

Striver's Row imprint before leaving to become the Publishing Manager of Amistad Press. He left Amistad after one year to become the first African American literary agent in the history of the William Morris Agency. Barron has formed his own literary agency, Menza-Barron, with Claudia Menza.

Herb Boyd is an award-winning author and journalist who has published 16 books and countless articles for national magazines and newspapers. His publications include *Brotherman—The Odyssey of Black Men in America—An Anthology* (One World/Ballantine, 1995), *Autobiography of a People—Three Centuries of African American History Told By Those Who Lived It (Doubleday, 2000); Race and Resistance—African Americans in the 21st Century* (South End Press, 2002); *The Harlem Reader (Crown Publishers, 2003); We Shall Overcome—A History of the Civil Rights Movement (Sourcebooks, 2004); and Pound for Pound—The Life and Times of Sugar Ray Robinson* (Amistad, 2005). His most recent book is the autobiography of music composer and musician Yusef Lateef (Morton Books, 2007).

Valerie Boyd is the author of *Wrapped in Rainbows: The Life of Zora Neale Hurston* (Scribner, 2003), the critically acclaimed biography of the novelist, anthropologist and legendary boundary-breaker. Former arts editor at *The Atlanta Journal-Constitution*, Boyd is currently an assistant professor of journalism at the University of Georgia. An accomplished writer, editor and cultural critic, Boyd has published work in numerous anthologies, magazines and newspapers. Her next book, *Spirits in the Dark: The Untold Story of Black Women in Hollywood*, will be published by Knopf in 2008.

Samuel R. Delany is the first African-American to distinguish himself as a critically acclaimed author of science and fantasy fiction. He published his first novel, *The Jewels of Aptor*, in 1962 when he was only 19, and by age 26, he had already won four

Nebula Awards. Delany's books provocatively explore themes of race, gender, sexuality, identity, freedom and power. His 1974 post-apocalyptic epic *Dahlgren* (now available in Vintage paperback, which has reprinted many of his novels) is one of the best-selling science fiction novels of all time. He has also written poetry, critical essays and several memoirs. Delany is a professor of English and creative writing at Temple University.

Tananarive Due is the author of seven books, including the American Book Award-winning *The Living Blood*. Publishers Weekly has twice named her novels among the best of the year, and recently she won the New Voice in Literature Award at the Yari Yari Pamberi Conference. Her supernatural thriller *My Soul to Keep* will soon be a movie from Fox Searchlight. Due co-authored *Freedom in the Family: A Mother-Daughter Memoir of the Fight for Civil Rights* with her mother, civil rights activist Patricia Stephens Due. She and her husband, Steven Barnes, recently sold their screenplay adaptation of Due's novel *The Good House*.

Linda A. Duggins is a Senior Publicist at Warner Books. As Co-founder of the Harlem Book Fair, she has helped to create a nationally recognized venue that promotes literacy and literary expressions with writers of the Diaspora. An avid booklover, she is the Co-leader of the African Diaspora Literary Group in New York City. Linda is also on the Board of Directors of the National Book Club Conference. Professor Henry Louis Gates Jr., Terrie Williams, Dexter Scott King and Deborah Mathis are among the many great authors represented by Duggins at Warner.

Tonya M. Evans is an attorney, performance poet, author of *Seasons of Her* (1999) and SHINE! (2001), and co-author of the *Literary Law Guide For Authors: Copyright Trademark and Contracts in Plain Language* (March 2003). She practices in the areas of public finance, intellectual property, literary law, and estate planning. Evans has contributed articles and reviews to *Black*

Issues Book Review, QBR The Black Book Review and *CLEO Magazine.* She owns independent publishing company FYOS Entertainment, LLC and maintains the following websites: www.ebelaw.net, www.fyos.com, www.literarylawguide.com, www.leapmembers.com

Christopher John Farley is the author of the best-selling biography *Aaliyah: More Than a Woman* and two novels, *My Favorite War* (Ecco Press, 1998) and *Kingston by Starlight* (Three Rivers Press, 2005). He is also coauthor, with Peter Guralnick, Robert Santelli and Holly George-Warren, of *Martin Scorsese Presents the Blues: A Musical Journey.* He has worked as an editor and pop music critic at Time and is now an editor at The Wall Street Journal. Farley's biography of the reggae superstar, *Before the Legend: The Rise of Bob Marley*, was published by Amistad/Harper Collins.

Marita Golden has distinguished herself as a novelist, essayist, memorist, and teacher of writing. Her writing and literary career has spanned over 30 years. Golden's fiction includes the novels, *After, Long Distance Life, A Woman's Place, And Do Remember Me,* and *The Edge of Heaven.* In the genre of nonfiction, Golden has edited two anthologies. She is author of *Don't Play in the Sun, Migrations of the Heart, Saving Our Sons: Raising Black Children in a Turbulent World* and *A Miracle Every Day: Triumph and Transformation in the Lives of Single Mothers.* Golden founded the Washington DC based African American Writers Guild and the Zora Neale Hurston/Richard Wright Foundation.

Linda Susan Jackson is deputy chair of the English department at Medgar Evers College, CUNY. She received a poetry fellowship from Cave Canem and published two chapbooks, *A History of Beauty* (2001) and *Vitelline Beauty* (2002). Her work has also appeared in the anthology *Streetlights: Illuminating Tales of the*

Urban Black Experience, the journal *African Voices* and Essence magazine. She is the author of the poetry collection, *What Yellow Sounds Like* published by Tia Chucha (2007).

Haki R. Madhubuti, one of the leading poets to come out of the Black Arts Movement, is a publisher, editor and educator. He has published 28 books (some under his former name, Don L. Lee) and is one of the world's best-selling authors of poetry and non-fiction, with books in print in excess of 3 million. Madhubuti is founder, publisher, and chairman of the board of Third World Press (1967), co-founder of the Institute of Positive Education/New Concept School (1969), and co-founder of the Betty Shabazz International Charter School (1998) and the DuSable Leadership Academy (2005) in Chicago, Illinois. He is the founder of the Gwendolyn Brooks Center for Black Literature and Creative Writing, founder of the Gwendolyn Brooks Conference, and director of the MFA Program in Creative Writing at Chicago State University. He is also a founder and chairman of the board of The International Literary Hall of Fame for Writers of African Descent. His most recent book is his memoir, *Yellow Black: The First Twenty One Years of a Poet's Life* published by Third World Press (2005).

Adam McKible is associate professor of American and African American literature at John Jay College of Criminal Justice, CUNY. In 2004, HarperCollins published Edward Christopher Williams's *When Washington Was in Vogue,* a previously lost Harlem Renaissance novel that McKible rediscovered. He wrote an introduction to the new edition. He is also the author of *The Space and Place of Modernism: The Russian Revolution, Little Magazines, and New York* (Routledge 2002). His essays on little magazines and on African American literature are widely published in anthologies, journals and reference works.

Susan McHenry is founding editor and editorial director of *Black Issues Book Review.* McHenry is also a contributing editor to

200

Contributors

Essence Magazine. A veteran magazine journalist, she has covered black literature, black authors and the publishing industry since 1977 and her reviews have appeared in such publications as *Ms. The Nation,* and *Newsday.*

Walter Mosely is the author of over twenty-three books, which cross the genres of mystery, speculative fiction, literary fiction, and nonfiction and many of which have been translated into twenty-one languages. His popular mysteries featuring Easy Rawlins began with *Devil in a Blue Dress* in 1990. Others in the series include *A Red Death, White Butterfly, Black Betty* and *A Little Yellow Dog* . *The Man in My Basement,* a novel of ideas set in contemporary time in a Long Island community, was published in January 2004. *Little Scarlet,* an Easy Rawlins novel set five days after the 1965 Watts riots, was published in July 2004 and became a recommended book for reading circles in Los Angles. In 2005, Walter published his first book for young adult readers, **47**, a mix of history, science fiction, and adventure. His most recent books are *The Wave* and *Fortunate Son.*

Elizabeth Nunez has just published her sixth book of fiction, *Prospero's Daughter* (Ballantine, 2006), which reconceives Shakespeare's *The Tempest* on a Caribbean island with growing tensions between the native population and the British colonialists. Her novel *Bruised Hibiscus* won an American Book Award. She is a CUNY Distinguished Professor of English at Medgar Evers College, where she chairs the English department. She also co-founded the National Black Writers Conference at Medgar Evers, CUNY in 1986 with her colleague and mentor, the late novelist John Oliver Killens, and also served as conference director during NBWC's critical first years. In addition, Nunez is co-editor with Jennifer Sparrow of the anthology *Stories from Blue Latitudes: Caribbean Women Writers At Home and Abroad* (Seal Press, 2006)

Emily Raboteau is an assistant professor of creative writing at the City College of New York. She has an M.F.A. in fiction from New York University, where she was a New York Times Fellow, and a B.A. in English from Yale. Her short stories have appeared in *Callaloo, the Missouri Review, the Gettysburg Review, Tin House,* and *Best American Short Stories 2003,* among other publications. She is the recipient of the *Chicago Tribune*'s Nelson Algren Award for Short Fiction, a Jacob Javits Fellowship, a Pushcart Prize, a New York Foundation for the Arts Fellowship and a Literature Fellowship from the National Endowment for the Arts. Henry Holt published Raboteau's first novel, *The Professor's Daughter,* in 2005.

Ishmael Reed is a novelist, poet, playwright, and the author of 20 books. He is also a publisher, television producer, editor of magazines and anthologies, and radio and television commentator. He is a founder of the Before Columbus Foundation, which annually presents the American Book Awards; the Oakland chapter of PEN; and There City Cinema, an organization, which furthers the distribution and discussion of films from throughout the world. His books include: *New and Collected Poetry*; the novels *Japanese By Spring, Mumbo Jumbo, The Terrible Twos, Reckless Eyeballing, and Flight to Canada*; and collected essays *Airing Dirty Laundry* and *Writin' is Fightin'*. In 1997, Viking published *MultiAmerica: Essays in Cultural War and Cultural Peace*, edited by Reed. In 2000, Basic Books published *The Reed Reader*, a collection of his writing including excerpts from all of his novels, selected essays, published and previously unpublished poetry, and two plays, *Hubba City* and *The Preacher and the Rapper*. In 2003, the Basic Books/Perseus published Reed's latest collection of essays, *Another Day at the Front*, Thunder's Mouth Press published *From Totems to Hip-Hop: A Multicultural Anthology of Poetry Across the Americas, 1900-2002,* and The Crown Publishing Group published *Blues City: A Walk in Oakland*. His online literary magazines, *Konch*, featuring poetry, essays and fiction, and *Vines*, featuring international student writing, can be found at www.ishmaelreedpub.com.

Carlos Russell is Professor Emeritus at Brooklyn College, C.U.N.Y. He is a poet, essayist and playwright whose plays have been produced at venues such as the Billie Holiday Theatre, the Brooklyn Academy of Music, the Amaturo Theatre in Ft. Lauderdale, the Shrine Temple in Tampa, and Creative Concerns in Brooklyn. Russell is former Ambassador to the U.N. and the O.A.S. for the Republic of Panama. He has served as Editor of the Brooklyn section of the *NY Amsterdam News* and Associate Editor of *Liberator Magazine.*

Carl Hancock Rux is a multi-disciplinary poet, playwright, performance artist and recording artist. His play *Talk* produced at the Public Theater in 2003 won an Obie award. He is the author of the novel *Ashphalt,* (Atria, 2004), which takes place in an urban dreamscape. Rux's poetry, fiction, and plays have been published in numerous anthologies. His collaborations include commissioned performances and operas with companies such as the Alvin Ailey Dance Company, Urban Bush Women, and the Bill T. Jones/Arnie Zane Dance Company. He is head of the newly formed MFA Writing for Performance Program at the California Institute of the Arts.

Robert Reid-Pharr's research areas are in African American literature and queer theory. He is the author of *Conjugal Union: The Body, The House,* and the *Black American and Black Gay Man: Essays.* His next work, tentatively titled "Once You Go Black: Desire, Choice and Black Male Masculinity in Post-War America" is a unique study of cultural and intellectual history in late twentieth-century America.

Sheree Renée Thomas is the editor *of Dark Matter: Reading the Bones* (Warner Aspect), winner of the 2005 World Fantasy Award, and the anthology, *Dark Matter: A Century of Speculative Fiction from the African Diaspora*, named a *New York Times* Notable Book of the Year and winner of the 2001 World Fantasy Award. Awarded the 2003 Ledig House/LEF Foundation Prize for Fiction and a New York Foundation for the Arts Fellowship, her work also has been nominated for a Rhysling Award and received Honorable Mention in The Year's Best Fantasy and Horror. Her stories and poetry appear in *Mojo: Conjure Stories, So Long Been Dreaming, storySouth, Bum Rush the Page: Def Poetry Jam, Black Renaissance*. She has a story forthcoming in *Afrofuture Females: The Blackness of Outer Space Fiction* edited by Marleen S. Barr.

Valerie Wilson Wesley is the author of the Tamara Hayle mystery series, as well as other noted works; her most recent novel is *Playing My Mother's Blues* (William Morrow, 2005). Her children's books include the Willimena Rules series published by Jump at the Sun. She is also the author of *Freed Freedom's Gifts: A Juneteenth Story* and a recipient of the Griot Award from the New York Chapter of the National Association of Black Journalists. Her first novel, *Where Do I Go From Here?*, was written in November, 1993 and received the American Library Association's "Best Books for Reluctant Readers" citation.

Nana Camille Yarbrough is the author of the award-winning children's classic, *Cornrows* and three other critically acclaimed books for young readers: *The Shimmershine Queens, The Little Tree Growing in the Shade* (Putnam) and *Tamika and the Wisdom Rings* (Just Us Books). Her album of poetry and music, *The Iron Pot Cooker* was released in 1975 and *Ancestor House*, a CD of original poetry and music was released in 2002 by Maat Music.